G000020499

SIMON CATLING'S
PLACING PLACES

THE GEOGRAPHICAL ASSOCIATION

THE SONG
THE BURNING SONG
THE DEMON VULTURES
THE HAZY TENTS   THE RAW
HORIZONS   THE DRUGGED SANDS   THE SCREAMING
THUNDER THE RATTLING BONES THE DUSTY MOUTHS
THE INFINITE EYES   THE DREAM POWER   THE CIRCLING
SKY THE TREACHEROUS BIRDS THE SHIFTING TOWNS   THE
SNARLING GUNS   THE BURNING STORM THE VAST RIVER THE
CLAY DANCERS THE BLACK MASKS THE RICH SANDS   THE HAZY
DEMON THE SCREAMING SKIES THE VULTURES MOUTHS THE RAW
EYES THE THUNDEROUS SONG THE SHIFTING TRACKS THE VAST
CIRCLE THE RATTLING BIRDS THE DUSTY TENTS THE GUNS SNARL
THE STEAMING HORIZON THE BONE FOREST THE BURNING TOWNS THE
SAND FLOWERS THE TREACHEROUS INFINITE THE BLACK TRACKED THE
DANCERS SCREAM THE MASKED GUNS THE THUNDERS MOUTH THE FOREST
TOWN THE CLAY HUTS THE STORMS POWER THE DRUGGED RIVER THE
SHIFTING SONGS THE SKYS EYE THE RATTLING DREAM THE SNARLING DUST   THE
SANDS DEMONS THE BURNING BIRDS THE CIRCLING HAZE THE RAW BONES THE
RICH TENTS THE SCREAMING FLOWER THE STEAMING CLAY THE BLACK SAND
THE MASKED   DANCE THE TREACHEROUS HORIZON THE STORMS TRACK
THE RIVER THUNDER   THE SHIFTY VULTURES THE
FORESTS POWER   THE RAW SKY THE SCREAMING
EYES THE DREAM SONGS   THE DRUGGED HUTS
THE HAZY TOWNS   THE BURNT CIRCLE   THE
GUNS MOUTH THE SNARLING BONES THE
INFINITE BIRDS   THE DUSTY FLOWERS
THE STORMS MASK THE THUNDERING
DEMONS   THE TENT DANCERS   THE
RICH CLAY   THE SHIFTED POWER
THE SANDY RIVER   THE BURNING
TREACHERY   THE RATTLING TRACK
THE BLACK STEAM   THE POWERFUL
DREAM   THE FLOWERING SONG   THE
DRUGGED STREAM   THE DANCING EYE   THE
HORIZONTAL HUT   THE MOUTHLESS   SNARLS
THE TRACKLESS SKY   THE RAW   FOREST
THE TENT TOWN   THE HAZY   RIVER
THE INFINITE SHIFT   THE   BIRD
STORM   THE TREACHEROUS   DEMON
THE BURNING DRUG   THE   GUN
DANCE   THE SINGING
BONE   THE MASKED
RICH   THE BLACK
CIRCLING   THE
VAST DREAM
SINGING

SIMON CATLING'S

PLACING PLACES

(SECOND EDITION)

Two hundred and twenty–six stimulating ways to
introduce children to locational knowledge

A resource for
primary and secondary
geography teaching

THE GEOGRAPHICAL ASSOCIATION

Acknowledgements

The author and publishers are grateful to the following for permission to include copyright material:

Dave Calder, for the Africa poem reproduced here as a frontispiece, and the map–poem of Antarctica on the Zenithal Equidistant Projection reproduced on page 50, both first published in *Continents*, 1981

The Controller of Her Majesty's Stationery Office, for extracts from *Geography for Ages 5–16*, 1990, reproduced on pages 6 and 55, and for the maps from *Geography in the National Curriculum (England and Wales)* reproduced on pages 13 to 20

© The Geographical Association, 1992, 1995

This book is copyright under the Berne Convention. All rights are reserved. Apart from any fair dealing for the purpose of private study, research, criticism or review, as permitted under the Copyright, Designs and Patents Act 1988, no part of this publication may be reproduced, stored in a retrieval system, or transmitted in any form or by any means, electronic, electrical, chemical, mechanical, optical, photocopying, recording or otherwise, without the prior written permission of the copyright owner. Enquiries should be addressed to the Geographical Association.

As a benefit of membership, the Association allows its members to reproduce material from this book for their own internal school/departmental use, provided that the copyright is held by the Geographical Association. This permission includes the maps in Chapter 3 and Appendix 3.

ISBN 0 948512 98 9

Design: Ian Chatterton

Cover illustration: Linzi Henry

Printed and bound in England by Stephen Austin & Sons Ltd, Hertford

Published by the Geographical Association, 343 Fulwood Road, Sheffield S10 3BP. The views expressed in this publication are those of the author and do not necessarily represent those of the Geographical Association. The Publications Officer of the GA would be happy to hear from other potential authors who have ideas for geography books. You may contact the Officer via the GA at the address above.

The Geographical Association is a registered charity – no. 313129

PREFACE

Preface to the first edition

There is a widely held view that knowing where places are is essential to the study of geography. There is also a view that helping children, explicitly, to learn where places are is an essential part of a balanced education. I share both of these views.

It is important that children develop a knowledge of places, and it is important that they learn how to use maps, atlases and globes. I agree with the argument that learning must go well beyond the rote memorising of locations and the simplistic use of skills unsupported by understanding; but I know of no geographer or teacher who would support such limited expectations of children.

There will always be arguments about which places might be put before children, and there will be differences of opinion about the points in their development when children might best be introduced to mapping skills. Maps, atlases and globes fascinate many children from a very young age. This curiosity must be sustained. In the teaching of geography, we must capitalise on this. To provide some ideas about how to do so is the purpose of this book.

It was germinated, unwittingly, by a conversation with Trevor Bennetts, then Staff HMI for Geography, on a train journey from York to London, when he wondered whether it would be possible to come up with 36 ways to teach locational knowledge. Little did he know what he had started! But I accept the sole responsibility for taking up the challenge and for going so far as to commit as many ideas for teaching as I could find to paper.

I hope you find it useful and have a little fun on the way.

Simon Catling, January, 1992

Preface to the second edition

This second edition has been prepared to take account of the changes to National Curriculum Geography following the Dearing review in 1994. The locational skills to be taught and the places to be learnt as points of reference have been amended in the light of the 1995 revised Geography Order. The opportunity has also been taken to redraft Chapters 1 and 2 and the figures, to integrate the postscripts into Chapter 3 and to make amendments to the appendices. Maps showing the location of the places to be learnt are included, as well as blank maps. Twenty–five more ideas for teaching locational knowledge have been added. The last one carries a health warning!

Simon Catling, June, 1995

CONTENTS

A KNOWLEDGE OF PLACES

*'...the study of geography should more particularly aim at leading pupils to:
a) acquire a framework of knowledge about locations and places that will help
them set local, national and international events within a geographical context,
and that will support their development of geographical understanding...'*
(DES/WO, 1990)

The placing of places

It *is* helpful when a place is mentioned – in the news, in a conversation (even if you have to ask 'where's that?'), in a book, or in other contexts – to be able to 'place' it somewhere in the world, however roughly. Having a sense of where other people are or have been, where events occur and where the places are that we encounter daily, personally or at second hand, confirms our own 'sense of place'. And it *is* useful to know how to find out where places are: what to consult or who to ask, and how to go about doing so. This supports our confidence in our own awareness of the world around us, and our sense of belonging within it, as part of the local and global family.

The purpose of this book

The purpose of this book is to support the development of children's personal knowledge of places and features around the world, to support their 'sense of place' in the world. It draws together a wide variety of activities to help children in primary and secondary schools learn locational knowledge. It also sets out to explain why a knowledge of places and features is valuable and to indicate some of the considerations that need to be given to the effective teaching of locational knowledge.

This introductory chapter establishes the need for map competence, and outlines the National Curriculum requirements of the four countries of the United Kingdom.

Chapter 2 considers some of the points you should bear in mind when planning your teaching of place knowledge. Why teach locational knowledge?

What issues should you consider? How should you approach teaching about places? What thought should you give to the images of places that such teaching will inevitably evoke? What do the children think?

The third chapter lists 226 ideas that you might find useful – depending upon your resources, schemes of work, personality, fitness, geo–political humour, experience, travel mania, media addiction, political correctness, wealth ... and the responsiveness of colleagues and the children! The ideas do not go into detail, they are intended simply to provoke thinking and imagination. They have been listed in a random order: partly because that is how they were gathered; partly because there is no set order in which to learn locational knowledge; but chiefly because it lets you create connections between ideas rather than having them imposed by predetermined groupings (though randomness can do that!), so you can work in the way best suited to the needs of the children, your resources, and your own preferences.

Some ideas are straightforward and self–contained; others are starting points for extensive investigative projects. Many, if not all, can be approached as problem–tackling activities. Some require limited effort; others are demanding. Some are simple; others are complex. Some require access to a good resource base; others test the ingenuity of the children (and teachers, parents, and anyone else who gets involved); some require no more than an atlas or a street map. Some will need time and concentration; others can be acquired through frivolous activity. Some have serious intent; others are just plain silly. What they have in common is the world and getting to know about the places in it.

There are many ways to build up locational knowledge. Hopefully, a few of the ideas in this book will strike a chord and provide a way in. A magic carpet is not included, but maps and atlases are a pretty good substitute for travelling the world. These ideas are just some of the ways you can make the journeys.

As a little light relief three other facets of locational knowledge learning are highlighted on pages 36 and 41. You will find that not everyone, in every school, is really good at learning where places are; symptoms of this sad condition are described in the notes on *locational knowledge deficiency*. Of course, you could end up at the other end of the spectrum, suffering from *locational knowledge dependency*. Ideas on how to overcome this compulsive urge are given in Chapter 3.

No publication on National Curriculum Geography would be complete without some idea of assessment levels on locational knowledge. On page 45 you will find the seven steps on the ladder to locational knowledge success!

Map competence

We cannot even begin to *know* where everywhere in the world is! So instead we learn how to *find* places: that is, we acquire the skill to read maps and find our way around atlases of all sorts. This skill is composed of ten competences. We need to be able to:

1 understand the title of a map

2 appreciate the purpose of the map

3 use the map key or legend

4 understand that the symbols used on a map show physical and human features

5 appreciate the extent and limitations of the information which collectively symbols give about a place or an area

6 locate places using grid reference systems

7 use compass directions on a map

8 know how to use the scale bar to measure distances and have some idea as to what these distances mean in reality

9 use the contents page to find relevant maps and information in an atlas

10 use a map index to locate places

The National Curriculum requirements for geography in England, Wales, Scotland and Northern Ireland make it explicit that children must learn the essential skills of map reading and use. Though the requirements are not identical, the overlap is clear. All the competences listed in Figure 1 need to be learnt by all children, whether or not they are listed in the National Curriculum of a particular United Kingdom country.

However, if we have no idea of the Earth as an entity and of some of the essential features of it, at both the global scale and locally, map competences will be used in a vacuum.

Acquiring a locational framework

The National Curriculum Geography Working Group for England and Wales stated in *Geography for Ages 5 to 16* (DES/WO, 1990) that a core dimension of children's learning of geography is their development of a 'locational framework', that is, a knowledge of where places are in the world. The English and Welsh National Curriculum Geography Orders (DfE, 1995a; WO, 1995a) require children to build up a *cognitive map* of the world which includes knowledge of where specified local, regional, national, continental and global places are. Each child is required to have a *common core* to her or his global cognitive map. This essential element in geographical awareness and understanding was also identified in the requirements for geography in Northern Ireland and Scotland (DENI, 1991a; SOED, 1993), though it was not set out in such an explicit fashion.

Though their approach is not identical – there is no National Curriculum for the United Kingdom – each of the Geography National Curriculum Orders for England, Northern Ireland, Scotland and Wales make it clear that children across the ages of 5 to 14 must develop their knowledge of places and features through their studies. They must also be able to locate places and features on suitable maps and globes. In England and Wales, National Curriculum Geography specifies places and features, or 'points of reference' as they prefer to call them, on several maps. In Northern Ireland some places and features are noted in the requirements, while in Scotland none are specified and the requirement relates to knowing places and features that are met in studies that children undertake.

Key stage 1 and its equivalent (5 to 7 year olds)

Children must be provided with opportunities to learn to:	England	Scotland	Wales	Northern Ireland
● use a globe and maps to identify major geographical features	✓		✓	
● identify land, sea, continents and mountains on maps and globes	✓		✓	
● extract information from globes, atlases and maps			✓	
● recognise the globe as a model of the Earth		✓		
● describe location by the use of letter/number co–ordinates			✓	✓
● use the four cardinal points of the compass				✓
● use letter/number co–ordinates to locate features on maps			✓	
● follow a route on a map	✓		✓	
● use globes, maps and plans at a variety of scales	✓			
● use maps, atlases, globes to develop an awareness of other places			✓	

Key stage 2 and its equivalent (7 to 11 year olds)

Children must be provided with opportunities to learn to:	England	Scotland	Wales	Northern Ireland
● use the globe as a representation of the world		✓		
● use relative location to interpret information on maps and globes		✓		
● use the key to interpret information on maps and globes		✓		
● use letter/number co–ordinates to locate features on maps	✓	✓		✓
● use four–figure grid references to locate features on maps	✓	✓	✓	✓
● use latitude and longitude to locate features on atlas maps				✓
● use the points of the compass to show direction	✓		✓	✓
● measure distance, using scale	✓	✓	✓	
● follow routes	✓		✓	
● use maps to find the location of features and activities	✓	✓	✓	
● use the contents and index pages to find information in an atlas	✓	✓	✓	✓
● use and interpret globes, maps and plans at a variety of scales	✓			

Key stage 3 and its equivalent (11 to 14 year olds)

Children must be provided with opportunities to learn to:	England	Scotland	Wales	Northern Ireland
● use keys in context		✓		
● use letter/number co–ordinates				✓
● use four–figure grid references		✓		✓
● use six–figure grid references to locate features on maps	✓	✓	✓	✓
● use latitude and longitude to locate features on atlas maps		✓		✓
● identify relief and landscape features	✓		✓	
● use the points of the compass		✓		✓
● use the contents and index pages to find information in an atlas		✓		
● follow routes	✓		✓	
● use and interpret maps, atlases and globes at a variety of scales	✓		✓	
● use atlases and a globe to find appropriate information	✓		✓	
● use thematic and specialist maps		✓		

Figure 1: The map competences to be used to locate places

However, for children in all four countries, the variety of places and features which they must know of and learn to locate include:

⭐ continents and countries

⭐ towns and cities

⭐ seas and oceans

⭐ mountains and deserts

⭐ rivers and canals

Children must also learn to locate features and activities in their local area and home region and in other localities and regions.

Figures 2, 3 and 4 list the places and features which children must have the opportunity to learn to locate as part of their 5 to 14 geography curriculum in England and Wales. Maps 1 to 6 show the location of the places and features to be learnt by children at school in England and Wales (DfE, 1995a). Maps 7 and 8 show the additional places and features to be learnt by children at school in Wales (WO, 1995a). It is worth noting, not quite as an aside, that the places and features on the 1995 maps of the British Isles, Europe and the World

have been modified since 1991! (Appendix 2 indicates what came and went.)

Children will be able to extend their cognitive maps beyond the required list of places through planned and incidental encounters with other places. This is the opportunity for children to *personalise* their cognitive maps.

Knowledge of the location of places is not confined to geography. The History Programmes of Study for key stages 2 and 3 specify a number of places which must be studied from a historical perspective (DfE, 1995b; WO, 1995b; DENI, 1991b; SOED, 1993). Work in history must include locating these places on appropriate maps. This, in itself, will extend the child's 'locational framework', which will be enhanced further when children encounter additional locations within their studies. Children will also encounter places in their work in music, art and other areas of the curriculum.

Creating and retaining a 'framework of locational knowledge' is required of every child. This was set out most explicitly in the original geography Orders for England and Wales (DES, 1991; WO,

---

Features and places which children must learn to identify on globes or maps as part of National Curriculum Geography in key stage 1 in England

Children must be provided with opportunities to learn to:

● locate and name on a map the countries of the United Kingdom

● mark on a map of the United Kingdom approximately where they live

Features and places which children must learn to identify on globes or maps as part of National Curriculum Geography in key stage 1 in Wales

Children must be provided with opportunities to learn to:

● identify Wales on a map of the British Isles

● show on a map of Wales approximately where they live

Features and places which children must learn to identify on globes or maps as part of National Curriculum Geography in key stage 1 in Northern Ireland

Children must be given a variety of opportunities to learn to:

● locate places they study in Northern Ireland

● locate the major physical features and towns of Northern Ireland

● locate places they study in the rest of the British Isles

● locate places they study in other parts of the world

Features and places which children must learn to identify on globes or maps as part of National Curriculum Geography in years P1 to P3 in Scotland

Children must be given a variety of opportunities to:

● develop a mental map of familiar places

Figure 2: Locational knowledge in geography to be introduced in key stage 1

1991) and hardly at all in the Northern Ireland and Scottish requirements (DENI, 1991a; SOED, 1993). For example, the 1991 Statutory Orders for Geography in England and Wales, in *Geography in the National Curriculum* (DES, 1991; WO, 1991) specified the levels at which assessment of locational knowledge should take place. The 1995 requirements are much more clearly in line across the four countries, with no specific reference made in the English and Welsh *Level Descriptions* to direct assessment of the places and features listed on the maps, which is also the case in the level requirements of Scotland and Northern Ireland.

Many children will develop their 'locational framework' effectively, but not every child will. One of the experiences waiting to be encountered by some children is deficiency in locational knowledge. This occurs when children find that they cannot remember all the places that they are supposed to be able to locate on maps. In teaching locational knowledge you must do all you can to support every child's development, and every achievement, however limited, must be acknowledged positively.

Conclusion

In summary, the requirements for developing knowledge of the 'points of reference' in the curriculum orders for geography in England, Northern Ireland, Scotland and Wales focus on the three key elements in locational knowledge:

 the **map competences** needed to be able to find and locate places and features on maps and the globe

 knowledge of our personal world, of our home area and the places and features important for daily functioning which are the core of our 'local' cognitive maps

 knowledge of the places and features that are specified in the national curricula that form a core for our 'global' cognitive maps

Wherever you go, however you travel and by whichever route, have fun 'placing places'.

References

DENI (Department of Education, Northern Ireland) (1991a), *Geography*, Belfast: HMSO

DENI (1991b), *History*, Belfast: HMSO

DES/WO (Department of Education and Science/Welsh Office) (1990), *Geography for Ages 5 to 16*, London: DES

DES (1991), *Geography in the National Curriculum* (England), London: HMSO

DfE (Department for Education, England) (1995a), *Geography in the National Curriculum* (England), London: HMSO

DfE (1995b), *History in the National Curriculum* (England), London: HMSO

SOED (Scottish Office Education Department) (1993), *Curriculum and Assessment in Scotland: National Guidelines – Environmental Studies 5–14*, Edinburgh: Scottish Office

WO (Welsh Office) (1991), *Geography in the National Curriculum* (Wales), Cardiff: HMSO

WO (1995a), *Geography in the National Curriculum* (Wales), Cardiff: HMSO

WO (1995b), *History in the National Curriculum* (Wales), Cardiff: HMSO

Features and places which children must learn to identify on globes or maps as part of National Curriculum Geography in key stage 2 in England and Wales

(i) Children must be given a variety of opportunities to learn to:

● use maps, atlases and a globe to locate places they are studying and that are in the news (Wales)

(ii) Children must be provided with a variety of opportunities to learn to locate the following places on globes or maps:

In the British Isles

Countries: United Kingdom; England, Scotland, Wales, Northern Ireland

Capital cities: London, Edinburgh, Cardiff, Belfast

Other towns (for children in Welsh schools): Swansea, Bangor

Mountain areas: Lake District, Pennines, Grampian Mountains, Cambrian Mountains **(and for children in Welsh schools):** Snowdonia, Snowdon, Brecon Beacons

Rivers: Thames, Severn, Trent **(and for children in Welsh schools):** Clwyd, Tywi, Teifi, Dee, Wye

Seas: English Channel, Irish Sea **(and for children in Welsh schools):** Bristol Channel, Cardigan Bay

Coast (for children in Welsh schools): Pembrokeshire Coast

Island (for children in Welsh schools): Anglesey

In Europe

Countries: United Kingdom, Republic of Ireland, Germany, France, Spain, Italy

Cities: London, Dublin, Berlin, Paris, Madrid, Rome

Mountain areas: Alps

Rivers: Rhine

Seas: Mediterranean Sea, North Sea

In the rest of the World

Continents: Europe, Asia, Africa, Oceania, Antarctica, North America, South America

Countries: China, India, Australia, Indonesia, USA, Canada, Russian Federation

Cities: Paris, Cairo, New York, Buenos Aires, Bombay, Sydney

Mountain areas: Himalayas, Rocky Mountains, Andes

Deserts: Sahara Desert

Rivers: Nile, Mississippi, Amazon

Canals: Suez Canal, Panama Canal

Oceans: Arctic Ocean, Pacific Ocean, Indian Ocean, Atlantic Ocean

Poles: North Pole, South Pole

Lines of latitude: Equator, Tropic of Cancer, Tropic of Capricorn

Lines of longitude: Prime Meridian

Features and places which children must learn to identify on globes or maps as part of National Curriculum Geography in key stage 2 in Northern Ireland

Children must be given a variety of opportunities to learn to locate:

● the continents and oceans

● the North and South Poles

● the lines of latitude, including the Equator and the tropics, and longitude, including the Prime Meridian (Greenwich), and the International Dateline

● the world time zones and time changes

● the major physical features of the British Isles and the rest of Europe

● the countries and major cities of Europe

Features and places which children must learn to identify on globes or maps as part of National Curriculum Geography in years P4 to P6 in Scotland

Children must be given a variety of opportunities to:

● extend their mental map to a wider area than places familiar to them

Figure 3: Locational knowledge in geography to be introduced in key stage 2

Features and places which children must learn to identify on globes or maps as part of National Curriculum Geography in key stage 3 in England and Wales

(i) Children must be given a variety of opportunities to learn to:

● use an atlas and a globe to locate places studied and places that are in the news

(ii) Children must be provided with a variety of opportunities to learn to locate the following places on globes or maps:

In the British Isles

Countries: United Kingdom; England, Scotland, Wales, Northern Ireland

Capital cities: London, Edinburgh, Cardiff, Belfast

Cities: Glasgow, Newcastle–upon–Tyne, Manchester, Leeds, Sheffield, Liverpool, Nottingham, Birmingham, Norwich, Bristol

Other towns (for children in Welsh schools): Aberystwyth, Bangor, Caernarfon, Llandrindod Wells, Newtown, Merthyr Tydfil, Newport, Swansea, Carmarthen, Wrexham, Mold

Mountain areas: Lake District, Pennines, Southern Uplands, Grampian Mountains, North West Highlands, Cambrian Mountains **(and for children in Welsh schools):** Snowdon, Cader Idris, Pen–y–Fan, Snowdonia, Brecon Beacons

Rivers: Thames, Severn, Trent **(and for children in Welsh schools):** Conwy, Clwyd, Dee, Wye, Usk, Taff, Tywi, Teifi

Seas: English Channel, Irish Sea **(and for children in Welsh schools):** Cardigan Bay, Bristol Channel

Coast (for children in Welsh schools): Pembrokeshire Coast

Island (for children in Welsh schools): Anglesey

In Europe

Countries: United Kingdom, Republic of Ireland, Belgium, Denmark, Sweden, Norway, Finland, France, Germany, Austria, Ukraine, Poland, Greece, Italy, Luxembourg, Netherlands, Portugal, Spain, Switzerland

Cities: Amsterdam, Athens, Berlin, Bern, Brussels, Copenhagen, Dublin, Helsinki, Kiev, Lisbon, London, Luxembourg, Madrid, Oslo, Paris, Rome, Stockholm, Vienna, Warsaw

Mountain areas: Alps

Rivers: Rhine, Danube

Seas: Mediterranean Sea, North Sea, Baltic Sea

In the rest of the World

Continents: Europe, Asia, Africa, Oceania, Antarctica, North America, South America

Countries: Algeria, Argentina, Australia, Bangladesh, Brazil, Canada, China, France, Germany, India, Indonesia, Italy, Japan, Mexico, New Zealand, Nigeria, South Africa, USA, Venezuela, Russian Federation

Cities: Beijing, Bombay, Buenos Aires, Cairo, Calcutta, Los Angeles, Mexico City, Moscow, New York, Paris, Sao Paulo, Shanghai, Seoul, Sydney, Tokyo,

Mountain areas: Himalayas, Rocky Mountains, Andes

Deserts: Sahara Desert

Rivers: Amazon, Mississippi, Nile, Yangtze

Canals: Suez Canal, Panama Canal

Oceans: Arctic Ocean, Pacific Ocean, Indian Ocean, Atlantic Ocean

Poles: North Pole, South Pole

Lines of latitude: Equator (0°), Tropic of Cancer, Tropic of Capricorn, Arctic Circle, Antarctic Circle

Lines of longitude: Prime Meridian (0°), 180°

Date line: International Date Line

Features and places which children must learn to identify on globes or maps as part of National Curriculum Geography in key stage 3 in Northern Ireland

Children must be given a variety of opportunities to learn to locate:

● features, environments and places they study

Features and places which children must learn to identify on globes and/or maps as part of National Curriculum Geography in years P7 to S2 in Scotland

Children must be given a variety of opportunities to:

● extend their mental map to areas met within places studied and the media

Figure 4: Locational knowledge in geography in key stage 3

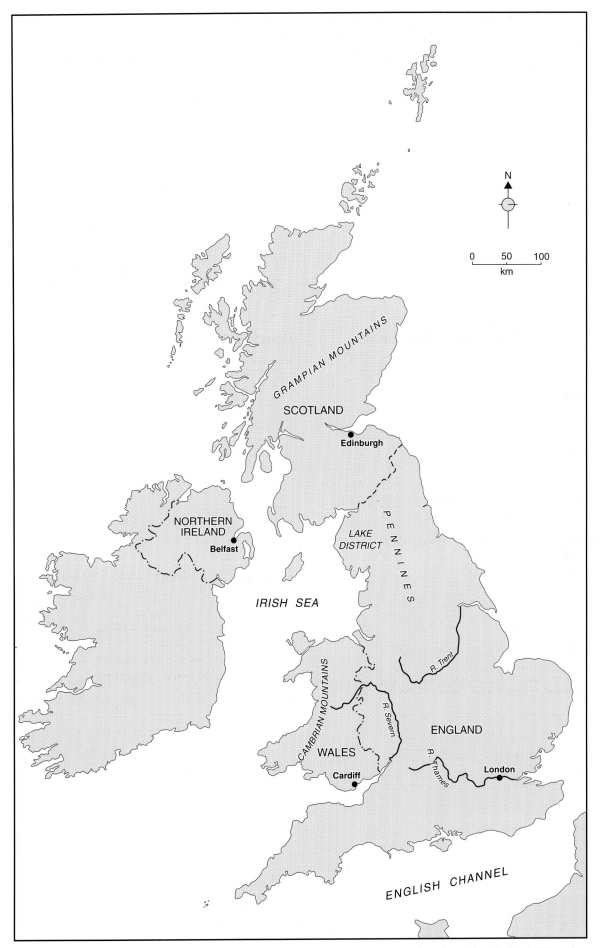

Map 1: National Curriculum Geography key stage 2 – the British Isles: the United Kingdom

Map 2: National Curriculum Geography key stage 2 – Europe

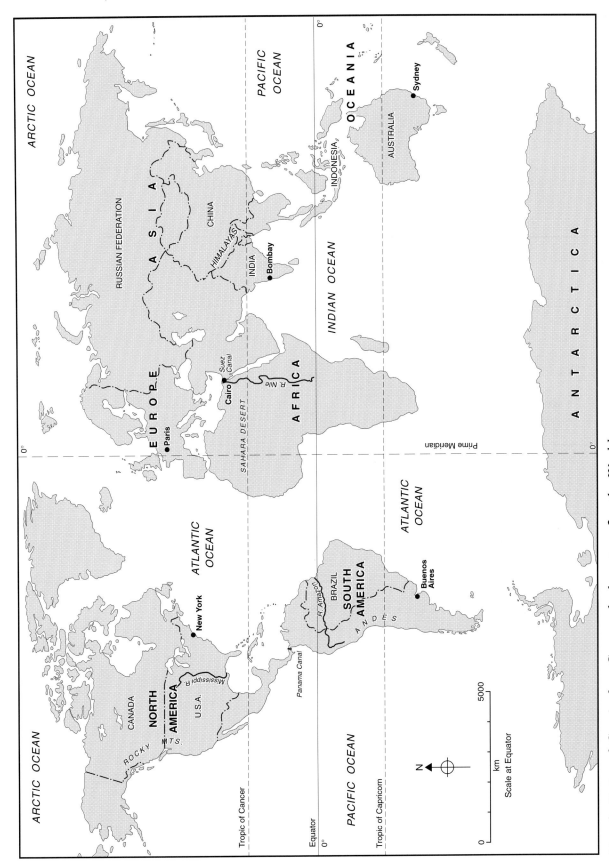

Map 3: National Curriculum Geography key stage 2 – the World

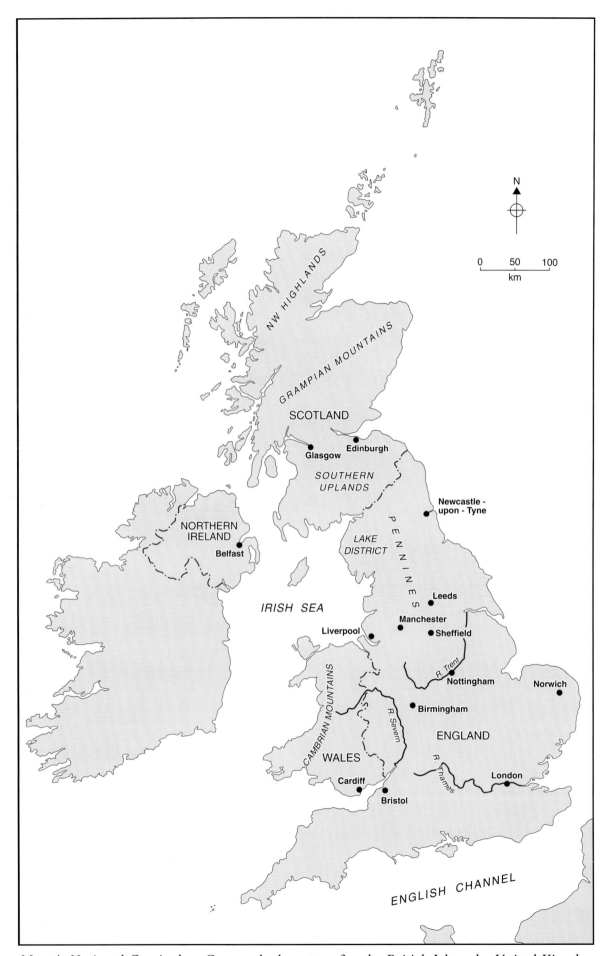

Map 4: National Curriculum Geography key stage 3 – the British Isles: the United Kingdom

Map 5: National Curriculum Geography key stage 3 – Europe

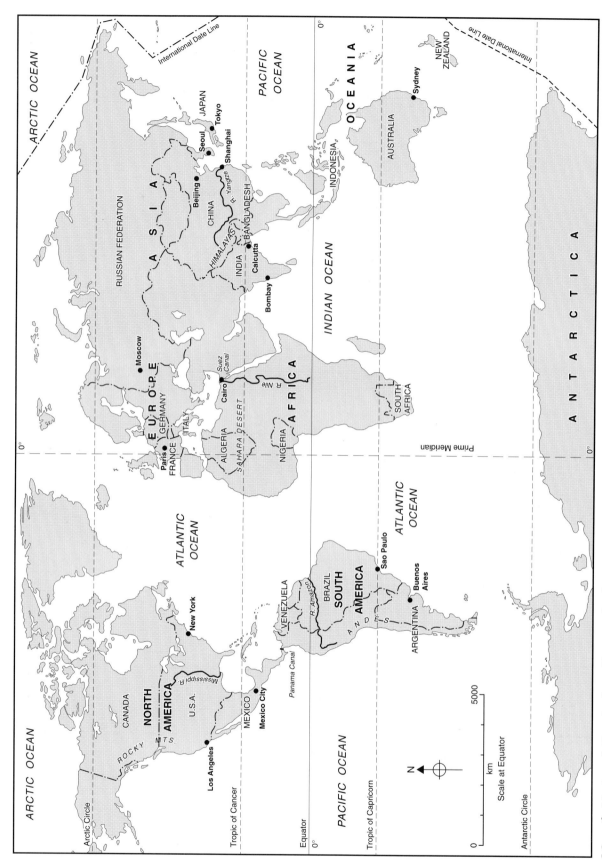

Map 6: National Curriculum Geography key stage 3 – the World

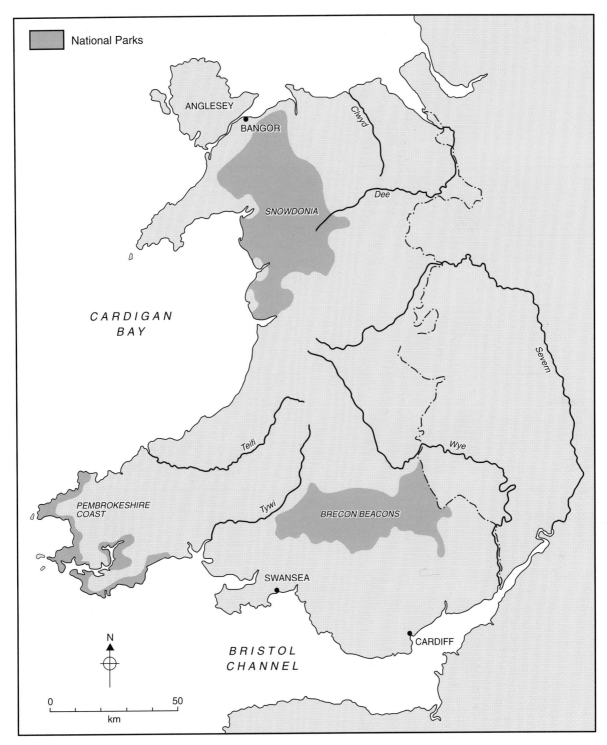

National Parks

ANGLESEY

BANGOR

Clwyd

SNOWDONIA

Dee

CARDIGAN
BAY

Severn

Teifi

Wye

PEMBROKESHIRE
COAST

Tywi

BRECON BEACONS

SWANSEA

N

CARDIFF

BRISTOL
CHANNEL

0   50
km

Map 7: National Curriculum Geography key stage 2 – Wales

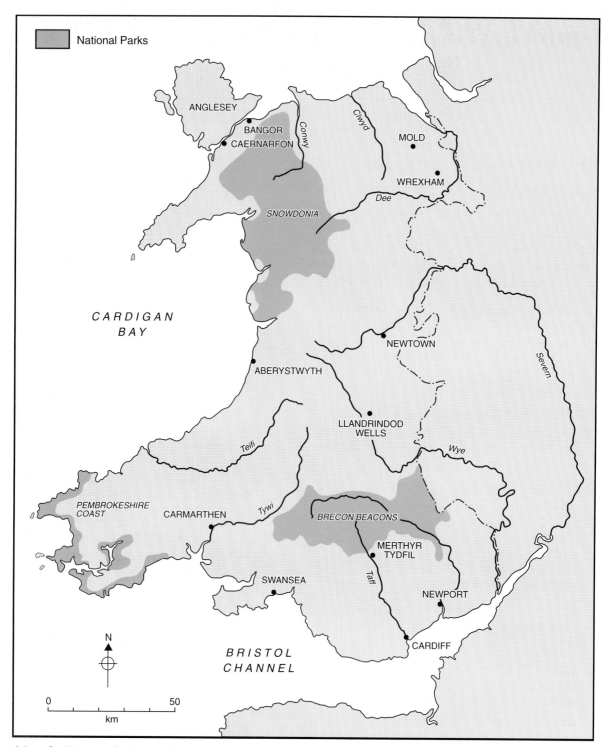

Map 8: National Curriculum Geography key stage 3 – Wales

TEACHING LOCATIONAL KNOWLEDGE

Why teach locational knowledge?

If all the understanding of geography which children take away from school is that it is 'about locational knowledge', then it will be a poor thing for them and of little value to others. Geography is so much more than that!

Teaching locational knowledge contributes to children's sense of living in the world, develops their awareness of the global environment and fosters their sense of responsibility as global citizens. It is a valuable contribution, for children with a limited sense of where places are have limited opportunity to see where their responsibilities lie and where their contribution to the future will have an impact. Justifications for teaching locational knowledge include:

- it fosters children's interest in places, a curiosity and fascination stimulated by what they hear, see and read;

- it widens their horizons, extending their partial awareness and helping them develop a global perspective;

- it develops their spatial awareness at a global scale, giving them a knowledge and sense of the Earth as a whole;

- it helps them develop a sense of scale, from the local to the global, of distance, and of globes and maps as representations, reductions and selections of reality;

- it helps them recognise the relevance of the rest of the world to themselves and their community and country;

- it gives them opportunities to develop an understanding of ideas such as similarity and difference, interdependence, pattern, scale, site, change, land–use, etc., to develop skills, for example in using atlases and reference material, comparing findings, developing enquiries, etc., and to examine values and attitudes about places, their nature and importance and their own images and preferences;

- it challenges the ignorance, partiality and bias which underpin stereotyping and prejudice, and developing an appreciation of the commonality and diversity of human experience of the Earth;

- it teaches them that their locational knowledge is limited – you cannot know where everywhere is – and that ignorance and bias can result from limited knowledge;

- it supports and develops their 'sense of place', which is fostered by the awareness of and knowledge about the wider world, enhancing their sense of belonging within the wider community.

Developing the knowledge, understanding, skills and values inherent in these aims for teaching locational knowledge is a long term process, and must be continuous throughout primary and secondary schooling. Though primarily the responsibility of the geography curriculum, geography does not provide the only opportunities to engage and encourage children in knowing about and knowing where places are. To make sense of history, to see art and music in context, to understand the sources of ideas in science, physical education and religious education, for example, it is important to have an appreciation of the *whereness* of the origin of ideas or the occurrence of events.

You need to adopt a planned approach to teaching about the location of features and places in geography and a common sense approach to recognising the opportunities that exist in other curriculum experiences for children.

Teaching and learning locational knowledge

The National Curriculum requirement for children to learn locational knowledge raises the question of how best to teach it. The Geography Working Group (DES, 1991, p. 47) commented that locational knowledge could be 'accumulated gradually through a variety of activities', including:

- the planning of journeys,

- games, jigsaws and quizzes,

- the use of computer programs about place knowledge,

- incidental references to globes and maps.

Planning effective opportunities for children to develop locational knowledge is important. If we are to succeed in helping children to build up cognitive maps of the locality, country and world, we must accept that it is important enough to demand the provision of active learning contexts and environments. We need to be well enough informed to be able to seize opportunities for learning as they arise – whatever area of work children are engaged upon at the time – and we must be able to draw upon a core of appropriate, up–to–date resources to use with the children.

Given that we have the necessary skills, knowledge, understanding and motivation, there are a number of factors that are essential for the successful teaching of locational knowledge:

- *planning opportunities into the curriculum* for the children to learn or to extend their skills in using and understanding of globes, atlases, maps, compasses, etc. through which they discover features and places;

- *using investigative projects* which involve children in finding out about places and the links between places;

- *making reference to places* in studies that are not directly place–based, recognising incidental opportunities as they arise;

- *including transition activities*, such as finding one or two places on the globe, in changing from one activity to another during the school day, as planned 'micro–tasks' with a single focus;

- *providing suitable resources* in the classroom, including a globe, wall maps of the British Isles, Europe and the world, a map of the local area, several different atlases for reference, computer programs, directional compasses, etc.;

- *displaying and ensuring access to these resources* for children, including the use of a display area to which the children can contribute and that reflects both their own place interests and other places of interest.

Criteria for selecting places to study

Although National Curriculum Geography requires the learning of particular locational knowledge, it is still important to bear in mind a range of criteria for selecting the places and features to be identified on globes and maps and for places to be studied. The Geography Working Group identified several criteria for the selection of the places and features given in the original Geography Order (DES/WO, 1990). SCAA also listed a variety of criteria, which were used in the redrafting of the map contents (SCAA, 1994). These are listed in Appendix 1. The criteria suggested here draw on and extend their work.

Locations and areas to study should be selected which:

- are appropriate to the understanding, experience and achievements of pupils;

- provide a balanced spread of awareness and knowledge about places around the world, enabling pupils to develop a coherent spatial framework of the world so they can relate newly encountered places to those known;

- are at a range of scales at one or more of which the focus of study and the depth and spread of enquiry are appropriate to the needs of the pupils;

- reflect current areas of interest around the world, including political and strategic significance and topicality of international events;

- reflect a balance of understanding and knowledge about the locality, home region, British Isles, Europe and the world;

- reflect similar and contrasting areas of the world to give a sense of global diversity, including environmentally, economically and in terms of population density;

reflect an awareness of places significant to the United Kingdom and the peoples within it;

 draw on teacher, parent, pupil and visitor expertise to provide insight into places and the value of place knowledge and understanding;

 build upon the available resources.

Approaches to teaching locational knowledge

Teaching locational knowledge must involve a balance of approaches. There should be rigour and challenge in the tasks set, but these must be stimulating and enjoyable. The serious study of places should be balanced by opportunities for a relaxed and 'fun' approach. As with all teaching, the need is to involve the children in active approaches to learning which draw on both first–hand and secondary sources, which use primary resources alongside material already selected by others, and which is not presented to children as the finished article but can be examined, analysed and challenged by them.

Approaches to teaching about locational knowledge should also reflect the following:

 the use of problem–solving approaches to learning, which should encourage children to develop skills in finding information as well as in identifying possible answers to the tasks set for them or by themselves;

 the use of enquiry methods in teaching, which should focus on encouraging children to pursue such questions as:

– do I know where this place is?

– what do I know of this place?

– what is my image of this place?

– how do I find out where it is?

– what can I find out about this place?

– what is this place like, and what is it like to be there?

– what is the limit of what I know?

– what do I need to do to find out more about this place?

 the use of entertaining challenges, which include such activities as quizzes, puzzles, jigsaws, crosswords, blank maps, charades, etc.;

 the use of cross–curricular skills involved in tasks such as:

– reporting the places mentioned in the day's news broadcasts and papers in various forms and for different audiences,

– identifying key sources for finding out about and studying places,

– using numerical skills to analyse the frequency of mention of places and to ask questions about the findings,

– storing and retrieving data about places using computer technology,

– making a presentation about why places become and sometimes stay worth knowing about.

The child's–eye view

If you focus on the value to the children of *knowing* about places, you will secure their interest in *learning* about them! Always encourage children to ask the question: 'Why is it important for me or to me to learn this location or about this place?' Discuss their responses to this question and examine such reasons as:

 it is an important place to me;

 to be well–informed gives me greater control over my life;

 there is a need to know what is going on in the world, and where;

 it is what is expected of 'educated' people;

 to understand and contribute to the world in which I live, I need to know about it, and that includes knowing where places are and how to find them;

 to appreciate what others are doing to the planet and to understand why others are concerned about this, among other things I ought to know where threatened places are;

 to challenge the limited awareness and images of places that I and others have.

Get the children to suggest places to be included within their personal and the class locational framework, drawing upon their own interest and engaging their sense of enquiry; ensure that they examine their own and each other's cognitive maps and place perceptions. Harness their knowledge; don't simply extend it!

The question of image

In teaching locational knowledge, we must recognise that images of places are being engaged and developed, some reinforced and some challenged. We may have little control over what really is learnt by children in school, of what remains with them, but it is in our control to do our best to foster a recognition of the extent and limitations of their knowledge and understanding of places. Stereotypes and misconceptions about places in the world are often based on ignorance and prejudice. Developing locational knowledge in children, as part of the contribution to developing their global 'cognitive map', can help to inform children as well as to help them begin to appreciate the bounds of their awareness. We should encourage children to keep asking questions, to retain a healthy scepticism and to want to find out more about places.

There are a number of points that need to be taken into account. First, to develop as broad a sense of the world as possible, children need to encounter and study a balanced range of representative places over their school careers. This has clear implications for planning the geography curriculum in both primary and secondary schools. Second, children's misconceptions about places must be examined and challenged, leading them to recognise the bias and limitations inherent in any set of knowledge, including that which is locational and place-based. So we must consider teaching approaches as well as geographical content.

Quite rightly, opportunities are taken to examine places and events that appear in the news bulletins in the press and on television. But topicality often means a focus on the dramatic or exotic to the detriment of 'ordinary' places that are mentioned just as often in the media. Third, then, we need to redress the emphasis on the dramatic by ensuring we find out about the 'ordinary' too. Fourth, there are dangers in characterising parts of the world as more interesting, developed or familiar because of the large or limited number of places learnt about in different regions, or through a focus on particular environments, products, ways of life, etc. The spread of places studied has an impact on our images of the world as a whole as well as on particular places.

There is, fifth, the danger of over-reliance on limited sources of information. This can be compounded by the use of out-of-date resources, whether globes or atlases, books or photographs or posters and study packs, which go unchallenged if they are not used critically alongside up-to-date resources. It is essential, though not always easy, to gather as wide a range as possible of useful and current resources in order to provide children with as accurate and informed a background as they can be given.

The support of the school

Though the teaching of locational knowledge is not a major aspect of geographical work, its successful implementation does place some responsibilities on a school. A fundamental need is to provide a range of suitable resources, which means that funds must be made available.

Within a school there should be a an up-to-date and accessible selection – if not all – of the following resources:

- inflatable globes

- stand–based solid globes

- floormat world and British Isles maps

- wall maps of the world, continents, countries and other places

- photographs of the Earth from space

- postcards showing views of the Earth

- jigsaw maps

- atlases for class and library use

- a CD–ROM atlas

- stencil and outline maps

- Ordnance Survey, street and other large–scale maps of local areas

- brochures and newspaper extracts

- books about places and the features of the Earth

- story books based on or referring to places around the world

- a collection of globes and maps as pencil sharpeners, on key rings, marbles, rubbers, etc.

- items from particular places built up from visits, visitors and purchases and requests

These resources should be available in the school library or resource centre, as well as in the classroom. They may take time to collect and up–date, but this should be provided for in the geography development plan.

As well as ensuring adequate resource funding, we should take advantage of opportunities to develop contacts with other parts of the home region, country and wider world, through parents, school links and local industries with national and international links as a way both to gather resources and to have real contacts with places. The cost in postage or through the use of the Internet can be included with other activities that use these resources.

Guidance on continuity and progression in the teaching of locational knowledge throughout the school must be included in the school or departmental curriculum policy for geographical work.

Schools also need to provide support and encouragement for the teacher–consultant with responsibility for geography and for the geography department staff to maintain awareness of current developments in teaching, to seek out more appropriate resources, to support colleagues in planning, teaching, assessing, recording and evaluating their geographical work, to develop an overview of the geographical work in the school and to foster the development of this area of the primary and secondary curriculum.

Assessing the understanding of locational knowledge

Though it does not do so directly, National Curriculum Geography nonetheless requires children's knowledge of the location of specified places to be assessed.

There are three points to bear in mind in the assessment of locational knowledge:

★ the school must have an agreed policy on the context of locational knowledge assessment: whether it is assessed discretely or as part of the children's wider geographical and other studies;

★ there must be agreement about the parameters for the accuracy of children's knowledge – that is, the 'zone of accuracy' on a particular type or scale of map that will be allowed – for their locational knowledge to be deemed achieved;

★ there should be a variety of acceptable ways for children to demonstrate the accuracy of their locational knowledge; for example, stating verbally or in writing where a place is, marking accurately on an outline map from memory the location of a place, or finding speedily on a suitable map a specified feature.

There is also the matter of recording children's 'achieved' knowledge of locations. One of the questions that has inevitably been raised is: how frequently does a child have to locate a place or feature accurately for it to be recorded that its location is 'known'? The common–sense answer must be that this approach is of no real value. If children can use the skills involved in locating places with a fair degree of competence and accuracy, they can have their competence in using map skills recorded (see Figure 1). If they show they are reasonably able to refer from memory to the continents and other major features and places on the Earth and can say where in the world places are which they are studying, you can record that children have this knowledge without the necessity to specify which places and features it is that they 'know'. Any record sheet should, therefore, list the map competences and refer to a general knowledge of locations.

Do not let this become a time–consuming and weighty matter. One successful approach is to involve the children in recording their own learning of places, from the earliest years. This gives them a responsible, proactive role in setting their own goals and recognising their own achievements. At the same time it gives you a clearer insight into the development of the children's knowledge, understanding and skills and the next steps to take. Work out with the children strategies that they can use themselves to record places and features they feel confident in locating and those they need to develop more secure knowledge about.

Sources of reference on the development of locational knowledge in the National Curriculum Geography in the UK

ACAC (1994), *Geography in the National Curriculum (Wales): Draft Proposals*, Cardiff: ACAC

CCW (Curriculum Council for Wales) (1991), *Geography: Non–Statutory Guidance*, Cardiff: CCW

DENI (1991), *Geography*, Belfast: HMSO

DES (1989), *National Curriculum Geography Working Group*: Interim Report, London: DES

DES/WO (1990), *Geography for Ages 5 to 16*, London/Cardiff: DES/WO

DES (1991a), *National Curriculum: Draft Statutory Order for Geography*, London: DES

DES (1991b), *Geography in the National Curriculum* (England), London: HMSO

DfE (1995), *Geography in the National Curriculum* (England), London: HMSO

NCC (1990), *National Curriculum Council Consultation Report: Geography,* York: NCC

NCC (1991), *Geography: Non–Statutory Guidance*, York: NCC

NCC (1993), *Geography in the National Curriculum* (leaflet), York: NCC

SCAA (1993), *The National Curriculum and its Assessment: Final Report* (the Dearing Report), London: SCAA

SCAA (1994a), *Geography in the National Curriculum (England): Draft Proposals*, London: SCAA

SCAA (1994b), *The Review of the National Curriculum: A Report on the 1994 Consultation*, London: SCAA

SCAA (School Curriculum and Assessment Authority) (1994), *National Curriculum 1995: Subject Seminars – Geography*, London: SCAA

SCAA (1995), *An Introduction to the Revised National Curriculum*, London: SCAA

SEAC (School Examination and Assessment Council) (1993), *Standard Assessment Tasks: key stage 1: Geography*, London: SEAC

SOED (1993), *Curriculum and Assessment in Scotland: National Guidelines – Environmental Studies 5–14*, Edinburgh: Scottish Office

WO (1991), *Geography in the National Curriculum (Wales)*, Cardiff: HMSO

WO (1995), *Geography in the National Curriculum (Wales)*, Cardiff: HMSO

References

DES/WO (1990), *Geography for Ages 5 to 16*, London/Cardiff: DES/WO

SCAA (1994), *National Curriculum 1995: Subject Seminars – Geography*, London: SCAA

TEACHING IDEAS

1 Watching wall maps

Put up world/continental/national wall maps around the school/classroom. List new place(s) to be found on the map(s) daily/weekly.

2 Addresses

Ask each child to write her or his address, including the postcode, the country and the continent. They should then draw a series of maps of decreasing scales to show the locations of the different parts of the address: their street, the town, the county, the country, the continent, the world!

3 Stamp and coin collecting

Collect stamps and/or coins from around the world and identify which nations they come from on world/continental map.

> A friend reports that only weeks after she had persuaded her 12-year-old to take up stamp collecting in an effort to improve a lamentable knowledge of geography she had asked "Where is Argentina?", the reply came – without a moment's hesitation – "Six pages after Chile."

4 Postmarks

Collect franked envelopes and identify on world/continental/national maps where they were franked.

5 Sponsored place competition

List a variety of places/locations to be learnt. Set a time limit for children to mark the places on a blank world/continental/national/local map. Children collect sponsor money for each place accurately located. Vary accuracy requirement depending on the age/experience of children.

6 Daily news

Using local/national newspapers and television/radio news broadcasts, find places mentioned using world/continental/national/local maps.

7 Balloon competition

Group/class/school children attach address label to own balloon. These are released. Request on labels to return them to the school stating where they landed. Find landing places on map(s).

8 Travel information

Collect travel brochures about places. Find out where they are, what they are like, how to get there. In a class, each child could collect information on a different place. All could be located on a wall map.

9 Case studies

Decide on particular places to study – village/town, area, nation. Groups/individual children find out all they can about the place(s), including location. Make a presentation about each place: display, book, orally.

10 Surfing the Internet

Using the Internet, make contact with a school elsewhere in the region/country/world. Exchange information about each other's area/nation. To do so work out best way to pass on information.

11 Pen–pals

Using contacts, aid organisations, Council of Europe, embassies, etc., obtain the address of a school in another part of country/world. Write to the school asking to set up individual/class/school pen–pal scheme. Through this exchange information about each other's area, lifestyle, etc.

Sponsored place competition (blank maps)

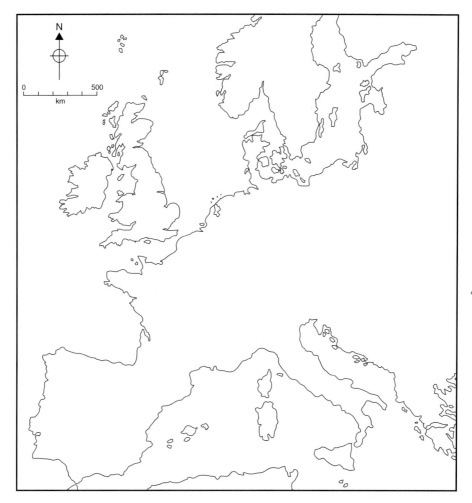

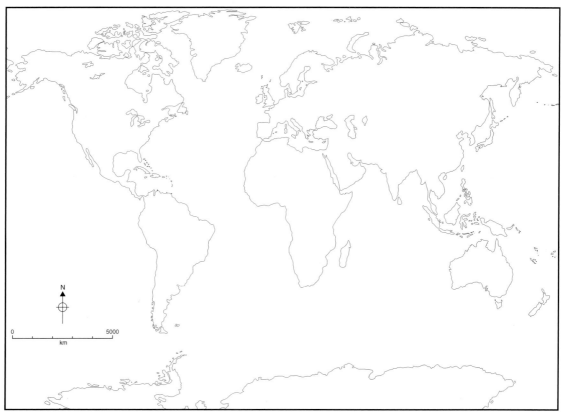

12 Search the atlases

Make a list of places to find. Using several different atlases see how many include the places on the list. Make a map to show which places occur in: all the atlases, several of them, one or two only, none at all.

13 Word search

Use word searches and blank maps. Children find the places in the word search. As each place is found its location must be marked on a blank map. Atlases/local maps can be used.

14 Using clues

Provide clues that help children to identify and locate places on maps. Children show/give grid reference/mark on a map the place they believe to be the correct answer.

15 Spin–a–globe

A plastic globe is placed on a table/floor area and spun round. A place that is uppermost/facing a child when it stops is noted and marked on a map.

16 Advertised places

Using adverts in newspapers/on television/in leaflets/on hoardings, find places that are mentioned on maps.

17 Play 'grid–ref'

Using a local map/atlas map which has letter–number/4 or 6 figure/longitude and latitude grid references, a child gives a grid reference which another has to use to locate and name the place. This can be played using two or more identical maps (by two or more children) along the same lines as 'Battleships'.

18 Pattern spotting

Shapes and patterns that can be found on a map are given to individuals or groups. These have to be identified on the map, by naming the place(s). Shapes/patterns could include continent/nation shape, river pattern, shape of upland area, settlement distribution pattern, etc.

19 Symbols

Using maps/atlases, find out how places are shown by symbols. These should include dots, lines, areas, numbers, letters and words, colours and shading. Examples of each could be identified on maps. Maps and atlases can be compared to see if common symbols are used or whether symbols vary according to map scale or publisher.

20 Tinned place

Collect tin cans with labels on them. Identify where each product was made. Find the location on national/continental/world maps. The names of places of origin/manufacture from large tins/cans that cannot be 'collected' can be noted and mapped.

21 Journeys

Follow journeys that are being or have been made around the nation/continents/world. Using maps mark the places visited or passed.

22 'Guinness' places

Using the *Guinness Book of Records*, find on a map the places mentioned under different categories. Thematic maps could be produced by 'record' category.

23 National flags

Collect national flags. Find the location of each nation on a world map. Make a wall map to show the country to which each flag belongs.

24 Going exotic

Children each select a place which they regard as exotic in some way. They must present their reasons and show where the place is on a map. These can be exotic local places or places elsewhere in the country/world.

25 Just like home

Find places elsewhere in the world that are very similar to the home area. Select criteria for judging their similarity. Show on a map where these places are. Individuals/groups of children could undertake this research.

26 Who's been where

On local/national/continental/world maps mark the places children in the class/ school have been/lived. This can be extended to include all adults working in the school, parents of children, and even anyone the children know.

27 The half–hour hunt

Give each child in the class the name of a place to find out about. They have half–an–hour to find out as much as they can and mark its location on a world map. Before selecting the places, check that information can be found on each one.

28 Sell a place

Children are given the name of a place they have to 'sell', perhaps to produce an advertising brochure. This must include its location. Different places are to be 'sold' by different groups of children. They judge which is the best 'sell' (other than their own!) when all have been completed and displayed.

29 Place classifications

Provide lists of places to individuals/ groups. They have to classify the places according to criteria they must justify. They also have to find out where the places are on a map.

30 Satellite photos

Children are given satellite photos or LANDSAT images and must identify the places they show using atlas/national/ region maps. They might draw an annotated sketch map to show the main features.

31 Jigsaw maps

Obtain jigsaw maps of countries/ continents/world for children to play with.

32 Make a jig–map

Children to select a local / regional / national/ continental/world map and make their own jigsaw map on card or wood.

33 Place mnemonics

Find place mnemonics from old geography textbooks to use to help children remember what is where. Children could also make up their own to try out on each other.

> Eating Wet Smarties Needs Intelligence, U Know
> England, Wales, Scotland, Northern Ireland,
> United Kingdom

34 Picture places

Collect photographs of places that show what they are like. Make picture books/ displays which include a map to show where the places are.

35 National collage

Collect photographs of a particular country. Make a collage within the border shape of the nation to show the nature and variety of life and environment.

36 Personalities and places

Choose/list from the press a number of famous people (in different walks of life and from different nations). Children must find out in which country each person was born, where they live currently and their nationality. The places linked to each person can be marked on a map.

37 Place matching

Put up maps and place names around the school/classroom. Children have to link the place names to the correct maps. This could be recorded on a chart or a base map can be used.

38 Passing through

Provide a list of rivers, mountain ranges, highways, railways, etc. that pass through several countries. Children have to identify/map the appropriate nations.

39 Cognitive maps

Ask children to draw a map from memory of the locality/country/continent/world, and to put in it what they know/like/think is there, etc. If several children draw cognitive maps of the same place, get them to compare what they have produced and consider why there are similarities and variations. These maps can also be compared with atlas map images. The children can look at the accuracy of their locations, how the information they have included differs from the atlas map, and how they can go about developing their cognitive map as a more balanced image of an area.

40 The Commonwealth Institute

If possible, take the children to the Commonwealth Institute (in London). Either focus upon one area of the Commonwealth or one country for study, or use the opportunity to find out which countries are members of the Commonwealth. Map where they are. Find out how the Commonwealth came into being and what its present role is.

41 Sponsored flights

Contact British Airways and other airlines, ask for information on their flights around the world. Ask if it is possible for a member of staff of one or more flights to become a contact for the class. They could send postcards, etc. from places they fly to and/or come to talk to the children about their journeys and the places they have visited. Why not try asking for a free flight, too?!

42 The assembly map

Using a wall map, refer to a place in the world in school assemblies. Ask children to find out about it over the next few days and to report back in a later assembly.

43 Presenting places

Ask each of the classes in the school to prepare an assembly about a place elsewhere in the world. Each class should focus on a different place. This could be done once or twice each term.

44 Befriend a place

Each week the class is to select a place, find out about it, and report to another class their findings.

45 Place a visitor

Invite an embassy official, someone known locally, a visitor through the Commonwealth Institute, etc., to your school to talk to the children about another country/locality.

46 Place books

Make a school/class/personal book of places based on a theme, such as 'places I like', 'places I hate', 'places I know of', etc.

47 Roll–a–globe

Using a plastic globe, roll it across the floor of the classroom / hall. Find which place is uppermost when the globe stops rolling. Mark it on a world map.

48 Make a globe

Using an old football, a balloon, paper or card, make a globe. On the globe mark any places you wish to include.

49 Make a wall map

Using an overhead projector or drawing freehand a class can make its own local/regional/national/continental/world map. On the map mark places of interest/known/liked/visited/heard of, etc.

50 The world outing

When on visits/field trips, set the children the task of collecting information (incidentally) about places elsewhere in the country/continent/world. These might include road names, advertising hoardings, travel adverts, etc. Back at school map the places noted and make a display.

51 In topic work

When undertaking a topic (either single subject or cross–curricular), include opportunities to refer to/find out about other places. For example, for 'Ourselves' look at 'my' connections with other places; for 'Vikings' examine their travels; for science topics find out where the originators of various theories lived/ worked; for art/music find out about the places where artists and composers lived and worked (especially if any of their work was inspired by a particular environment or place).

52 Time zones

Find out what the time is in other parts of the world at a given time here in the UK. Select a place elsewhere, give the time there. Find out what time it will be in other named places around the world.

53 Time travel

Find out how long it takes to travel to different places around the country/ continent/world. Compare different forms of (mixed) transport. List places that have to be travelled through. See which of two routes to the same place might be the quickest route and why.

54 Weather world

Use weather information to see what the weather is like in different places nationally/continentally/globally. Make seasonal comparisons.

55 Global climates

Find out about world climates, the variety and the variations within 'climatic belts' and map them. Identify places that typify the climatic region, and places that do not, within the same area, indicate why.

56 From outer space

Imagine yourself as a visitor to Earth from another star system. Make a record of the places you visit, those that interest or frighten you, etc.

57 Mythical origins

Find out the origin of myths/legends/folk tales/fairy stories, etc. On a world map locate the place where the tale is thought to have originated and other places where it is known to be told. Similar maps can be created for stories/novels, poetry, and varieties of music and art.

58 Mapping war and peace

Create a map of places around the world where there are armed conflicts/ non–violent conflicts. Map places which appear to be at peace. Decide on the criteria to use to select such places.

59 Language in place

Map the variety of languages used in the locality/home region/nation/continent/ world. Map the spread of these languages.

60 Place names

Select a variety of places around the continent/world. Find out how the names are spelt/written/pronounced in the national/local language. Compare these to the version that is used in a British atlas.

61 Games time

Play board/tactic/chance games like 'Diplomacy', 'Monopoly', 'The Weather Game', 'The Underground Game' or 'Where on Earth' in which real places are the backdrop to the game.

62 Where do I know?

Unannounced, ask the children to list as many places as they can (eg towns/countries/rivers, etc.) in a given time limit, perhaps 2/3 minutes. Alternatively, give them a blank map and ask them to mark on it as many places as they can in a set time. Afterwards, the children should check their accuracy with a local map/atlas, etc.

63 Projection comparisons

Obtain a variety of world map projections (eg. Mercator, equal area, Peters (see below and opposite). Get the children to compare the projections, looking for similarities, variations, distortions, etc.

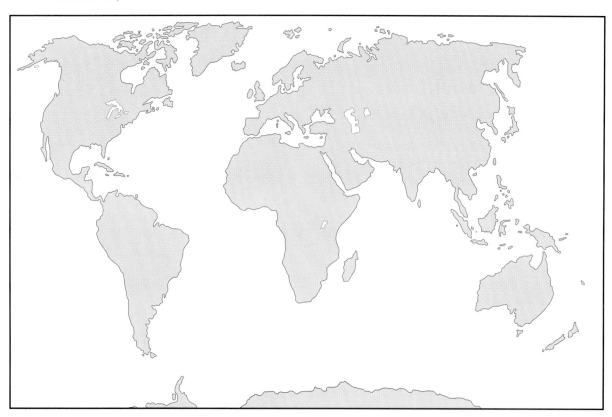

Mollweide's projection

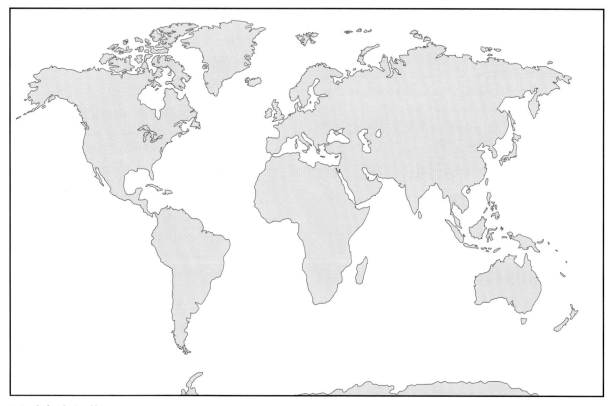

Modified Gall's projection

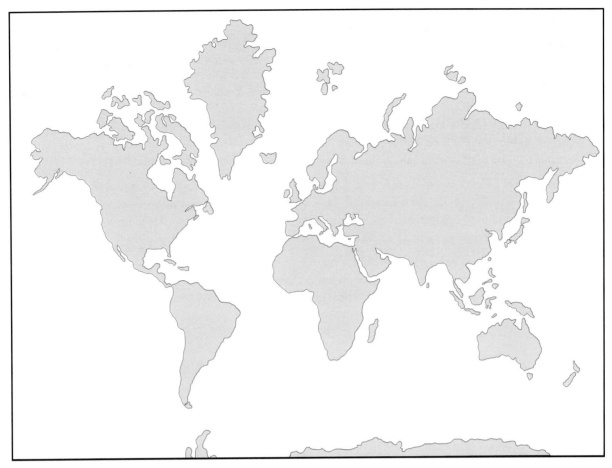

Mercator projection

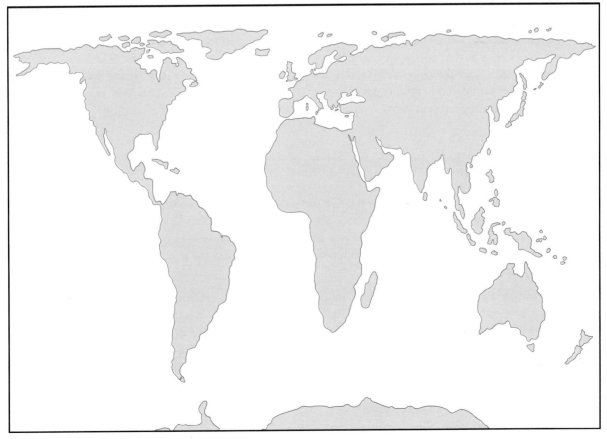

Peters' projection

Locational knowledge deficiency

For many children the requirement to retain a predetermined set of national and global 'points of reference' in their heads will be demanding enough. Identifying these features and places on the globe or suitable maps may well be too much for some children. Because locational knowledge will be assessed in some form, some children will be found to be deficient. For those for whom this is a serious matter – in that they find it hard to recall or point out the majority of the places specified – there is the danger of being labelled as suffering from 'locational knowledge deficiency'. This needs to be recognised as a form of special educational need and supported as such.

Where a number of children in a class or a school suffer from 'locational knowledge deficiency' there is the strong possibility of the class or school developing 'locational knowledge deficiency syndrome'. Even taking account of the active work of teachers, the likely knock-on effect for a school in this situation is a damaging outbreak of 'locational knowledge deficiency neurosis'.

A school in this state will need considerable support, particularly in-service courses on the teaching of locational knowledge in order to help children understand where they are, identify where they need to get to, give them the guidance to support their journey and find ways that let them know when they arrive and that the effort was worthwhile!

64 Locate the animals

Visit the nearest zoo to the school. Find out which animals are kept there and the place of origin of their species/breed. Map these locations on a world map. Alternatively, do the same using a book about animals.

65 Comparing areas

Using tracings/cut outs, etc. on graph paper (ie. all at the same scale) compare the areas of different countries/continents. Find out which are the largest/smallest. Put those being compared in rank order of area largest to smallest or vice versa.

66 Word world

Find out the place of origin of names found in the local area, eg. words used in daily conversation/names in recipes. Consider how and why this might have come about.

67 Play 'boundaries'

Each child in a group has an identical atlas open at the same page, showing one continent on which national borders are marked. Children are asked to name one nation which is bordered by a set number (eg. three, six, none) of others. They can also name the nations bordering a particular country.

Locophobia

It is well to be aware of the worst state that an individual can reach when suffering from 'locational knowledge deficiency'. This is the state of 'locophobia', the fear of learning where places and features are. Mild locophobics merely shudder at the utterance of place names or the giving of locations, whereas those with the worst symptoms run tearful and fearful from the sight of globes or maps, often in the wrong direction.

The only known treatment for sufferers is to place them in an environment free of all locational information and media, a state known as 'suspended cartography', in which no references to places are encountered. Clothing labels have to be removed, and none can be worn on which places or their names are displayed. Books, TV, radio, travel posters, papers – indeed, anything that might contain a reference to places must be removed, even Jaffa oranges – such is the anxiety their presence can induce in locophobics.

In the past it was thought that cases usually occurred in conjunction with 'mad curriculum disease', but more recently support for this theory has waned.

68 A dot–to–dot world

Provide dot–to–dot outlines of countries/ continents for children. First they must write down the area they think is shown, then join up the dots, and finally identify the place.

69 Tracing places

Children create their own map of an area (eg. region/nation/continent) from whichever sources they wish to use, presenting it as neatly as possible. It should also be as accurate as possible, so tracing from an atlas map is to be encouraged.

70 Old worlds

Using out–of–date atlases children can be asked to find out which countries were part of the 'British Empire', which were dominions/colonies/protectorates (and what these terms meant), which parts of the world used to 'belong' to which European nations, and for how long. They could then discover how and why the situation changed. Historical atlases can also be used in this activity.

71 Make a place capsule

As a class select places to be included in a time capsule. Decide what information is to be included about the places and map them. Put the map in the capsule with all of the other information and bury it!

72 Point the way

Using a compass, orient an atlas map in alignment with the world. Help children find out where they are on the map. Ask them to work out the correct direction to particular places around the world, then to point in that direction from where they are. Have a globe available. Consider what the difference is between pointing in a sideways directions to places on the other side of the earth and pointing downwards to the floor, and why both can be valid.

73 Theme maps

Select particular themes (eg. population, economic crops, transportation systems). Make national/continental/global maps to show the distribution/variation of the theme. Describe what the map shows.

74 If only we could travel

As a class map those places which everyone would like to visit if they had the opportunity. Collect information/pictures/ maps of the places included. Make a display.

75 Images of my world

Each child imagines they are a 'national' of a particular country. They must find out what the images are that 'foreigners' hold of that nation and present them as a display. The display should also include the image that the 'national' of that country would wish to present.

76 Abbreviated places

Provide children with a list of abbreviated names of places, they must discover the full name. Alternatively a map with abbreviated names on it could be used. Abbreviations can include shortened names and initials.

77 Place ephemera

Make a collection of 'disposable' items, eg. fruit labels, sweet wrappers, paper/plastic wrappings, newspapers. These items should include the name of the place of manufacture/origin or which come from another part of the world. Map the origins of the goods collected.

78 Globe tossing

Using a plastic inflatable globe, children toss it to each other. The thrower calls out the name of a place shown on the globe which the receiver must find before tossing the globe on in similar fashion.

79 Eating places

Find out about where the ingredients in school meals or in packed lunches originates. Discover the favourite meals of the children. Map the locations from which the recipes originate.

80 Place spotting

Call out the names of places for children to find. They must find the place in an atlas as quickly as they can, and mark it accurately on a blank map. Alternatively, atlases can be open at a specified national/continental map; children put up a hand to show they have found it; someone may be called out to point out the place on a wall map.

81 Channel places

Encourage children to tune into foreign radio stations. Set the task of identifying the language, finding the country of origin and mapping them. Discover in which languages and to which countries the BBC broadcasts; map them. (Encourage the school to buy a receiver dish if need be!)

82 A place a day ...

Every day each child must find a new place of their own choosing in an atlas, record it on a map they are making to show their chosen places, and do their best to remember its location.

83 The European World

Make a series of maps to show how the world was 'discovered' by European explorers.

84 Early maps

Make a collection of early maps of nations/continents/the world. These should include copies of maps made in/from other parts of the world (eg. Chinese, Inuit, Egyptian). Consider how the areas are shown, comparing them with satellite photos and modern atlas maps. Look for accuracy and discrepancies.

85 Predicting places

Make one or more maps predicting which places the children think will be in the news 1/5/10/25/50/100 years from now. Request reasons for the choices.

86 Place a present

Give the children a map/atlas/globe as a leaver's gift or just for fun! They're worth giving to someone.

87 Computer maps

Play any one of the variety of computer games that uses maps of the UK/continents/world. Consider why the places included have been selected, what the purpose and value of the game is, how it could be improved (or whether it is beyond help), and what can be learnt from it. Review a variety of programs using criteria to identify which is felt to be the best/worst.

88 Data maps

Using computer programs create data bases or maps to show selected place information, for example, a computer atlas, that can be both used as a source of place location information and be added to.

89 Wear the world

Wear a T–shirt/sweater/pair of tights/ Bermuda shorts which have maps/place names on them. Encourage people's interest in them. Get the children involved in printing/knitting/ embroidering their own.

90 Badge maps

Set up a mini–industry project to make badges in the shape of local/national/ continental/world maps. Make samples, undertake market research, produce and sell the products. Keep a record of the parts of the world that sell best/worst.

91 Playground maps

Have maps of the locality/home region/ country/continent/world marked on the school playground. Significant features (mountain ranges, rivers, etc.) can also be marked.

92 Multinationals

Make contact with companies which trade internationally. Find out where they originated. Discover the extent of their international trading. Map the information gathered. Predict where they might expand. Invite a member of the company to talk to the class about their international links and to send postcards to the school when on any overseas trips.

93 'Trivial Pursuits'

Play 'Trivial Pursuits'. Focus especially on answering the 'geography' questions. Make a list of all the places mentioned. Produce a map to show those you knew in 'right' answers and those you 'knew' in wrong answers. Decide which is the most/least trivial.

94 Locational mobiles

Cut out shapes of nations/continents. Hang them as mobiles in the classroom.

95 Places in courses

Plan geography courses that introduce children to the world as a whole and to areas and places in the world that are important. Use clear criteria for the selection. Such courses must involve the consistent use of maps to encourage children to learn locations of places.

96 Place quizzes

Send children home each Friday with either a blank map on which they have to mark named places or a map on which they have to name the places marked. The completed work should be checked on Monday.

97 Board maps

Children make a cheeseboard/clipboard/ tray in the shape of a country/continent they selected. It must be of a suitable size and made to be used.

98 Place map mats

Buy dining table place mats printed with maps. These can be used by the children at meal times. Make up sets which show different nations/continents, etc.

99 'Feely' maps

Make tactile maps for young children to play with. They can be of parts or the whole of the world. Encourage children to name the shapes correctly. Play 'feely' games by putting several shapes in a bag; the children must feel the shapes and name each one correctly before taking it out of the bag to check.

100 Sand maps

Use sand or earth trays (or the sandy sea shore/a patch of bare earth) and draw the shapes of places or routes. Children have to identify the area, they should use maps/atlases to help them. Children, in groups, can take turns in this activity.

101 Global change

Develop a study project in which children have to find out about the changes going on around the world. These might be political, environmental, technological, social. They should discover what is happening, where, when, why and to what effect. Mapping the findings should form part of the results of the study.

102 National snap

Make two sets of playing cards. On one set draw maps of countries, on the other write their names. The game is played according to the rules of 'snap'. (Snap can be called and the pile collected when the map/name of a country are put down consecutively.)

103 Map snap

Make a set of cards which contain maps of countries, country names, names of capital and other cities, and the names of rivers and mountain ranges. Put a world map on a table which shows some, but not all, of the places in the card set. 'Snap' can be called when a place on the card is spotted on the map. For the pile of cards to be collected, the caller must locate the place on the map immediately.

104 Changing names

Find out about the past name of as many places as you can, eg. Zimbabwe (Southern Rhodesia), London (Londinium). Locate these places on a national/continental/world map. Find out when and why the names changed.

105 Going round in circles

Using a globe follow 'great circle' routes between two places. Identify the places in between on the 'great circle' route.

106 Think latitudinally, or longitudinally speaking...

Follow a line of latitude or longitude on a globe or world map. List the places (areas, seas, nations, towns, rivers, mountains, etc.) through which it goes. Make a strip map of the places by the line of latitude/longitude.

107 Taping places

Record the names of countries and capitals, continents and countries, continents and rivers/mountain ranges, etc. onto a cassette tape. Listen to it in order to help you memorise this place information.

108 Daily places

Identify days which have special significance for particular places, eg. 23 April (St George's Day) for England; 4 July (Independence Day) for the USA. Make a world map which shows these places and a book which explains their significance.

109 How far apart?

Make a chart to show the distances between selected places around the world. Provide a world map to show the location of the places.

110 Placing the 'Worldwise Quiz'

Using the GA's 'Worldwise Quiz' booklets, map the locations of all the places mentioned. Find out which parts of the world seem to be well/poorly represented. Ask the compilers why this is so. Provide them with some ideas about what to ask in future to ensure a balanced representation.

Overcoming locational knowledge dependency

Being interested in where places are is healthy. But, like anything else, it can be overdone.

The result of becoming too absorbed in learning where places are – for teachers and children – is a compulsion to keep on learning the locations of new places, becoming ever more obsessed by the acquisition of place knowledge. When this stage is reached, the patient can be said to be suffering from 'locational knowledge dependency', a condition whose main symptom is 'locational acquisitiveness'. In its acute form, the sufferer becomes unable to stop telling other people where places are or to keep pointing out places on globes or maps to them.

There is no certain cure for locational knowledge dependency. However, a few potential remedies are being trialled.

Possible treatments for locational knowledge dependency

1 Deflate–a–place
Buy an inflatable globe (or several if a severe case). Pin flags into as many places on the globe as possible before it deflates. Focus on places that are best forgotten first.

2 Forget–a–place
Select a place to forget. Concentrate on forgetting that place for a day, then two days, and so on, until recalling the place to be forgotten becomes impossible.

3 Place tests
Give daily tests on lists of places to be located on blank maps. The aim is to get fewer correct each day.

4 Why?
Whenever anybody mentions a place, instead of asking where it is, ask why it is necessary to know about the place, let alone its location. Make no effort to find out or remember the location of a place which anyone mentions.

5 Placelessness
Create a geography course which makes no reference to real places, indeed no places at all.

111 Memory maps

Using whatever method is preferred, learn the location of as many places around the world as possible. Aim to be able to locate on a map any place mentioned and state where a place or feature is when asked. After all, it's what geographers can do; it's their 'party piece'.

112 What a relief?

Choose a certain height above sea level. On a large–scale/atlas map children must find places that are at, above or below this height. They could also find the highest capital city, the lowest local street, etc.

113 Famous places

Make a list of places that are well–known for some reason, eg. Venice and Birmingham for canals. Make a picture map (national or global) to show their location.

114 Team places

On local/national/European/world maps mark the locations of teams which play football, cricket, hockey, baseball, ice hockey, athletics, tennis, etc., be they local or national, amateur or professional. Find out why these teams exist, what has led some to become well–known, some nations to be ranked or perform so much better than others.

115 Notorious places

Make a list of 'dangerous' places ... at your peril! eg. the Bermuda Triangle. Where are they? Map them. Why are they regarded as 'dangerous', 'scary', 'to be avoided'? They might be local places which people stay away from, or they might be places elsewhere in the UK and the world.

116 Leisure places

Where do people go to 'get away from it all', for a day out/for a weekend break/to play sport/to relax with family or friends? Survey families, teachers, others who work in the school and people you meet in the street. Map the places they go regularly, infrequently and annually. Compare what you find with the advertising literature about where to spend your leisure time, whether it's a night out or your annual holiday.

117 Story places

Many stories and novels, for children and adults, are set in real, even if somewhat disguised, places. Select a story which refers to places that can be identified and use maps to find them. Follow the action in the story and work out whether it is based on an accurate knowledge of the places.

118 Placing a tale

Encourage children, when developing their own stories, to base the events in real places and to use maps when drafting their tale. They may well need to obtain other information to help them, eg. rail timetables, about one–way streets, building use.

119 Save–a–place

Where are those places/environments about which there is pressure to conserve/preserve for future generations? These may be local places, e.g. some woodland; or places of global importance, eg. Antarctica. Identify and map them. Illustrate the map with captions about the value of their conservation.

120 Who knows where it is?

Devise your own place quiz. Survey your friends/children in other classes/people in the street. Ask them to identify from a map (or to mark on it) the location of a variety of place: cities, nations, rivers, mountains, etc. Make charts to show how well different groups of people do, and to show which places the groups know best/least. What conclusions do you draw from this?

121 Signposting

Choose places of significance, whether local, national or global. Find out in which compass direction the places lie. Either make one or more signposts to stand in your classroom or hang signboards from the ceiling (include metric or time distances on the boards – with a note on what type of transport is being 'used').

122 Correct–a–trail/ Fail–a–trail

On a world map outline a famous journey, ancient or modern, but ensure that it is inaccurate in places. Give a group of children the task of discovering how accurate it is. They must then produce an accurate map of the route.

123 How big is your place?

Ask the children to select a city/region/nation and to find out its size. They will need to decide on criteria for 'size', eg. area, population. Individuals or pairs should select different places of the same type, eg. countries, so that they can compare the 'sizes'. They can consider why there is variation in size. Present their findings as a display.

124 Topophilia/Topophobia

Where are the places you love and hate? Indicate why you feel this way about them. Create a display to show what attracts you to certain places (topophilia), and what repels you from others (topophobia); make a map to show where they are.

125 Places past and present

Using sets of current resources and of out–of–date resources (textbooks, atlases, posters, photo packs, encyclopedias, etc.), either find the places – towns, regions, nations, physical features – most/least frequently mentioned or those given most/least space. Mark these locations on two separate maps and give reasons why some places appear on both maps and why others appear on one.

126 Inaccurate maps

Provide copies of national/world maps which contain inaccuracies. Ask groups of children to check the accuracy of the maps and to correct any errors they identify. They must produce evidence to show why they believe their correction to be more accurate. Lead into a discussion about problems in making maps that are absolutely accurate.

127 'Seeing' the world

Take two old (or new!) copies of the same atlas, cut out the maps and fit them together. Select the largest scale map of each area shown and make a world map using them. Place next to it an equal area world map. Consider what arises from what you have done (apart from anger for having cut up atlases!). What images of the world do atlases present? Try doing the same thing with two copies of an atlas from another country; what is presented as their view of the world?

128 Locating reporters

Where do newspaper/television/radio correspondents report from? Where are they based? Which places do they visit? Using newspapers and magazines, television and radio news reports over several days, map the locations and movements of reporters. Identify why the reports come from these locations.

129 Blowing hot and cold/ getting wet or dry

Make a map to show places that are at the extremes of climate and weather. Discover reasons for these extremes.

130 Regional images

Regions or areas around the world are often referred to in conversation and by the media, eg. the Middle East, Central America, the North East, the Sun Belt, the Steppes. What images do they conjure up? When are these titles used? Make national/continental/world maps to show the location of these regions.

131 Mural maps

Make maps part of your school environment. With help from local artists/art college students, design and paint maps on classroom/corridor/ playground walls showing the locality/ local region/nation/world.

132 A global connection

Build up a collection of globes, of all types, shapes and sizes: inflatable and solid, ancient and modern, from pencil–sharpeners to table–lamps. Do they all show the same places? What variations are there? Why? Which might be the most useful globe(s) for finding out about places? Why?

133 The 'ephemeral' globe

Globes, pictures of globes, and hemispherical maps (showing one half of the Earth) appear on all sorts of objects, including balls, pencil–sharpeners and placemats. Make an exhibition of globes to illustrate the variety of contexts in which the Earth appears. Consider why globes are used in this way.

134 Sizing up maps

Use maps which show countries/regions/ oceans/continents, etc. at the same scale and with the least distortion of shape. Cut out, for example, a number of countries (or seas, mountain chains, continents), and overlay smaller countries onto larger ones for a sense of comparative size. Give reasons why some countries are so much larger or smaller than others. Locate small or large countries on a map and see if any patterns emerge.

135 Map grids

How many different types of grid reference systems are used on maps? Find a variety of local places and some from elsewhere in the world which you can locate on maps using different grid systems. Give a variety of grid references for each place.

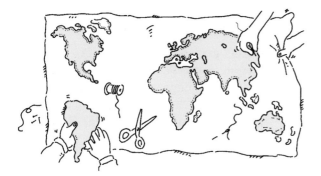

136 World blanket

Make a blanket which incorporates a patchwork map of the world. Similarly, make a patchwork map of the local area, UK, Europe or any other place/area.

137 World basket

You have been shopping, list and map the places where the products came from. This may need further research, for example supermarket chain products often give the head office of the company not the place of origin. Can you find out enough to make two maps: one showing where the raw materials came from (eg. where the beans were grown) and the other showing the place of manufacture of the product (eg. tinned baked beans).

138 Symbolising places

How are places shown on maps? List a number of places that you know of locally/ nationally/globally. Using a variety of scales and types of maps which include these places, record how they are shown. Give reasons for the variety of ways in which maps of different scales and purposes show places.

139 Nickname maps

Many places have nicknames, eg. New York is called The Big Apple. Make national/world maps showing places only by their nicknames. Children must identify the real names of the places.

140 Right sites

Where are strategically important places? What are strategic sites? Why are they important (whether for defence, commerce, access)? Find out about sites/cities/regions/ nations that are/have been strategically important. Map the location of the sites and indicate what is significant about them. Give

further information either on why they became (and remain) important or why their importance diminished.

141 Atlas collecting

Collect as many atlases as you can (buying them from jumble sales, secondhand bookshops, car boot sales, etc.) Make a display of them. Compare what they show. Look for changes to places, different styles of presentation, variations in content, difference in emphasis depending on the age group aimed at, etc. Compare the way the same place is shown in as many different editions/types of atlas as possible.

142 Collage world

Cut up old atlases to make a collage map of the world (it must show the shape of the world accurately). However, the shape of each continent must be made up of maps of countries which do not belong in that continent. Once the map is made the correct national boundaries must be drawn over the collage continents. What impression is made?

143 How many thematic maps?

Collect from current/old atlases as many different thematic maps as possible of a nation/continent, eg. physical/political/ climatic/trade/transport/disease/ population. Which types of thematic map occur most frequently? Which nations/ continents are represented most often?

144 Place–a–car

Provide a group of children with photographs of a variety of cars, lorries or motorbikes, and a national/European/ world map. The task is to make a display which shows from which countries the makes of car originate. Such a display can be created with any type of product with a variety of manufacturers from around the world.

145 Others 'discovered' our world

Make a world map to show how the Earth was 'discovered' by non–European people, eg. Chinese. Consider what sort of evidence will be needed; be prepared to use your evidence to infer what the extent of their world knowledge may have been.

146 Unknown places

Identify a place which you believe no one else in the class knows about. Make it known to them. You should teach them where it is, what it is like, how you get there, and so forth. Work out how you will do this, remember to include various maps.

147 Trading places

Where are a particular nation's/the world's major ports? Are they the same ports as 50/100/200 years ago? Why have there been changes? Have shipping routes changed? Why has this occurred? Mount a display to show the developments in trade around the coasts of countries and between the ports of nations around the world.

Children must know their place!

Seven steps in assessing the quality of children's place placing

It is important to know that children can place their places accurately. The notes below are offered as a guide to identifying children's achievement. However, you must decide what will suffice for you to credit a child with having learnt where a place is.

step	associated behaviour
0 No understanding ...	Child unable to point even in the direction of a globe or map. Usual responses include: 'The what?', 'What's that?', a blank stare as though you are speaking another language or come from a foreign country.
1 A glimmer of experience...	Child waves a hand in the direction of a globe or map. Usual responses include: 'It's over there ...', 'It's over there?', 'I think it's that thing ... the whatsit ...', accompanied by a waving of the hand in the generally correct direction.
2 The barest essentials of understanding ...	Child recognises that you need to look at the globe or a map of some sort. Usual responses include: goes in search of globe or a map of some sort and brings it back, saying 'It's on here ... somewhere ...', waves hand vaguely over the correct hemisphere (almost).
3 Almost there ...	Child goes to a globe or map straight away and brings it to you (or you to it). Usual responses include: moves hand in the correct general area, saying 'It's somewhere around here', and is getting close.
4 Spot on ...	Child goes straight to globe or suitable map. Usual responses include: points immediately to the named place or feature, saying 'It's here', and is correct!
5 Really has got it ...	The child knows exactly whether you need a globe or a map, and which map. Usual responses include: the hand shoots out with the finger pinpointing the exact location, so fast that you know she did not really need to look, saying 'It's right there.'
6 Understands, to the extent that ...	The child simply takes charge! Usual responses include: the child responds saying, 'That's the globe (or, over there is the map you will need). Would you fetch it.' (Which you do.) 'Now, can you find ... Look south (that's down; don't worry) then east (your right). It's at latitude ..., longitude ..., though it is hard to see on this globe (or, map). Well done, Miss (or, Sir). You are there.' To this the bemused teacher probably replies, 'Thanks Sharon. I wondered where my holiday villa is. Can you tell me what it is like there. I'm a bit unsure what to take or do ...' To this, Sharon responds, 'Oh yes, Miss (or, Sir). I'd say that you need to take ...' In the end the teacher gets Sharon to book next year's holiday, the school journey ... and buys shares in Sharon's company 'PLACES – Where we don't know isn't there'!

148 Places are index–linked

Provide children with a variety of atlases. Give them the index reference for a place, but not its name. Their task is to find the place in the appropriate atlas, both on a map and in the index.

149 People as places

Find towns / rivers / countries / islands/ mountains / deserts, etc. which are named after people. Who were the people? Why were their names given to these places? Choose a category (eg. towns named after people) and map their distribution around the world. From which part of the world did most of the people come? Why is this?

150 Desecration maps

Where are the most damaged places on the Earth's surface (eg. the Dustbowl in the USA)? Identify and map places and areas that have been permanently damaged by human action and examine how this occurred.

151 Frequenting the atlas

Select a particular atlas. Which places are mentioned the most (regardless of which scale of map they appear on)? Find out how often the UK and other nations are identified. Make a chart to indicate the number of different maps each place appears on.

152 Clues to places

Provide children with various clues about a place or particular feature on the Earth (eg. island, mountain, city, sea). Their task is to identify the particular place or feature and locate it on an appropriate map.

153 Fantasy locations

Identify from books/films, etc. places which are imaginary but nonetheless sited in real parts of the world. Map the rough 'location' of these fantasy places. Which are the real places 'near' the imaginary ones?

154 Significant places

Which places are significant to you/classmates/other children/parents/ teachers/ other adults? Plan how to find out. Make maps and charts of the results of surveys. Compare what has been discovered, and explain why there may be variations between different groups of people.

155 Catastrophe mapping

Maintain an up–to–date world map of disasters that occur round the world. Mark the places on the map, indicating the type of disaster and whether it is natural or the result of human action. Keep a cuttings book of articles about the disasters clipped from newspapers. Occasionally mount a display to show what is occurring where. Identify any patterns that may emerge.

156 Starting with a blank map

Provide children with a 'blank' map of a part of the local area/a country. Ask them to add as much information to it as they can to inform someone about that area. They must have a purpose in mind, eg. for a touring holiday, and may use any resources they are able to find.

157 Happy maps

Map places in which happy experiences have occurred for people (eg. holidays, fun events, peace breaking out). Draw on a range of sources, including the people in the school, their families, reports in the media and from books/magazines.

158 Making your own 'Worldwise Quiz'

Using information you gather about places make your own quiz to try out on other children. Organise a competition in class/school between groups who would like to participate. Include different categories of knowledge about places to find out which team has the best all–round knowledge. If you have enjoyed it, why not enter the GA's annual Worldwise Quiz competition?

159 Paper places

Use all of the newspapers from one day and compare the frequency of mention of places in the UK, Europe and the rest of the world. Make similar comparisons using English language editions of foreign newspapers. Compare the mention of local places in different local newspapers.

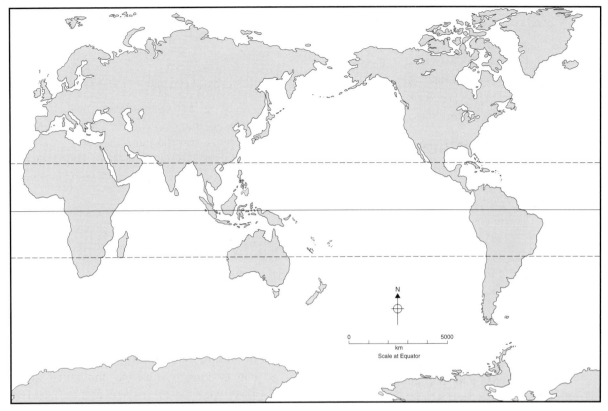

An Australia-centred world map

160 Centre World

Most world maps that we see have the UK and Europe in the centre. Ask the children to select a place elsewhere in the world, whether a city, country or continent. They must make a world map centred on that place.

161 Freehand mapping

Ask children to draw their own maps freehand using one or more maps of the area/country/continent as a source.

162 Community connections

Find out how the local community is linked to the wider world. Map a variety of the connections (eg. nearby towns on local signposts, the links to national or multinational shopping chains and other companies, restaurants which have origins elsewhere in the world).

163 Hunt the nation

Provide unlabelled outlines (or cutouts) of countries. Pupils must use an atlas or globe to identify the country from the shape. A pair of children could be given say ten countries to identify within a time limit, eg. ten minutes.

164 Souvenir places

List typical souvenirs which visitors or tourists might bring home from trips to other places. Make a map to show places where these souvenirs might be bought. Make both national and world maps.

165 Monumental places

Many monuments have been built in places around the world (eg. Nelson's Column in London, the Eiffel Tower in Paris). Map the locations of famous monuments around the world.

166 My favourite place

Where else in the locality/the UK/the rest of the world would you like to live? Prepare a report with a map to indicate where it is, and give reasons for your choice.

167 Collect a continent

Gather as much information about a continent as you can from the resources provided, and make a book. Different groups could work on each of the continents.

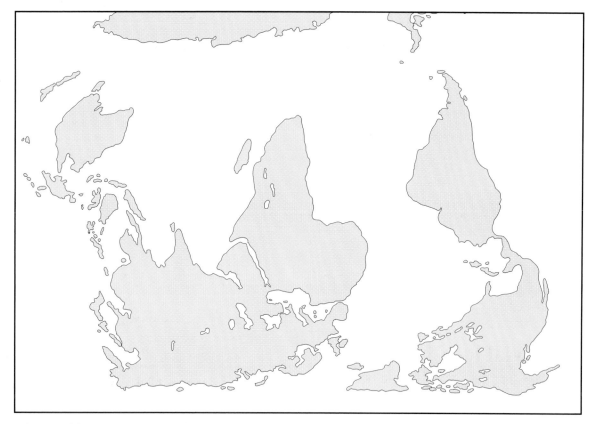

The World: it all depends on how you look at it!

168 A world turned upside down

Provide a map of the world in which Antarctica is at the 'top' of the page; give it a title to ensure that the children use it this way up. Ask the children to annotate the map, naming continents, oceans, mountains, major countries and cities, rivers, seas, etc. Allow them to use 'conventional' atlases for guidance. Discuss how they feel about making and using the map. This could be undertaken as a class activity or done by groups of children or individuals.

169 Travellers' tales

Use extracts from the writings of people who have travelled the country, continents and world. Ask the children to find the places mentioned in the diaries/journals/ books and to map the journeys; they could also show how the travel was undertaken.

170 Nursery places

On a wall map mark the places named in nursery rhymes and playground rhymes, songs, etc.

171 Folk spots

Collect folk stories from different parts of the world. Map their places of origin.

172 Mapwords

Make up a crossword using the names of places around the country/continent/world. Provide a map on which the clues replace the place and feature names, which the children must identify in order to complete the crossword.

173 Connecting places

Using a range of travel maps, shipping/rail/ road/air routes/ canals/rivers/ footpaths, play a game in which groups of three or four children are given the names of 10–20 places. They must work out an order in which the places can be visited; it must be possible to travel to each one directly from the previous one (to accomplish this the children must use the maps provided). Different groups of children can be given the same list of places, and they can compare their final sequences. To make it more demanding the children must end in a particular destination or fulfil certain criteria en route.

174 Place pursuit

Within a specific time limit set children the task of marking 26 places on a blank map of the country/continent/world, each place must begin with a different letter of the alphabet. Different criteria could be used to make the task more challenging. They may use atlases.

175 Place inversion

Draw a map of an island/country/ continent, but invert the relief features of the area, so that highland becomes lowland, lakes become hills or mountains, etc. Ask individuals or groups to give these features names which are anagrams of the proper names of the real features. Provide maps to help the children undertake the task.

176 Trivial locations

Make up quiz questions in which the answers are places. The clues should be varied, ranging from 'name the country X is in' through 'which place is associated with this person/activity?' to 'give the location of Y feature'.

177 Play 'location'

This game is based on the twenty questions approach. Someone thinks of a place; the class/group has to try to identify it by asking location questions. The person answering the questions must say how accurate the location question is.

178 Cartoon places

From newspapers / magazines / comics collect cartoons that include references to places. Include political/satirical cartoons as well as joke ones. Map the places that are mentioned. Does a pattern emerge? Can it be explained? Discuss the images the cartoons present and their accuracy and fairness.

179 Round the World in 80 locations

Plan a journey round the World. Select 80 specific places to visit and plan the sequence in which to visit them. Use as many different means of transport as you can, but only one between two locations.

180 Place a joke

Try to find/make up jokes/humorous comments about specific places (be careful not to give offence). Make a book in which these places are listed and shown on maps.

181 Make a 'Map Fact' book

Create your own book which gives up-to-date information about places/ environments. Decide on the criteria, that determine what to include and what to leave out, before you start.

182 Itinerary

Select 20–30 places on a national/ continental/world basis and write each on a separate piece of card. Give the set of cards to a group of children. Their task is to work out a sequence in which they will visit the places and how they will travel from one to the next.

183 'Personalising' maps

Prepare an outline map of the country/ continent/world. See how many places you can find which have the same names as children in your class/school. Mark all these places on the map.

184 'I've been everywhere!'

Remember that song? Make up a song/ poem/doggerel/limerick which includes the names of as many places as possible, rhyming the lines using place names. Individuals or groups could compose their own verses, and should provide a map to show the location of the places mentioned.

185 Stereo–locations

Find pairs of places with the same name in different parts of the country/world. Discover as many pairs as you can. Research why these pairs have the same name. What variety of reasons are found? What does this explain about how places acquire their names?

186 Placing stereotypes

Name a place or part of the world, eg. Paris, Holland. Ask children to write down 5/10/15 words about the place which come to mind. What sort of image do the children have? To what extent is it stereotypical? Undertake a project which examines the influences which shape the image, and which provides the opportunity to modify their image of the place.

187 National match

Provide children with separate lists of countries and capitals in random order, and with a suitable atlas. Their task is to match each capital to its country. As children become proficient, set time limits. Other pairings can be used, eg. rivers and continents, products and countries.

188 Twenty questions

Provide two to four children with a copy of the same map/atlas. One child selects a particular place, eg. a feature/city/country. The other children have to work out which place by asking fewer than 20 questions, to which the must answer 'yes' and 'no'. Encourage the children to play the game several times to work out which are the most useful questions.

189 Make your own atlas

Either by drawing your own maps or by cutting up an atlas that you bought at a jumble/car boot sale, create your own atlas. Decide which places to include, the order they appear in, etc. Make a contents page and an index for key places. Write an introduction to the atlas with reasons for your selection.

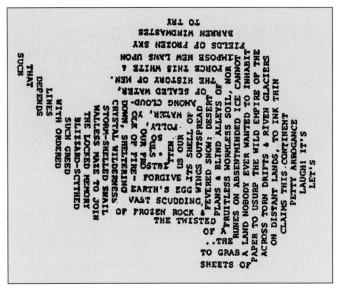

A place poem: Antarctica by Dave Calder

190 Shaping ideas about places

Write a poem/story/description, make a collage, paint a picture about another place in the shape of that place – use the shape of the streets of a locality, the shape of a town boundary or the shape of a continent.

191 Atlas workbooks

Use an atlas workbook with an atlas to help children develop an understanding of how to use an atlas, picking up locational information as they work through it.

192 Make a place diary

Ask the children to keep a place diary for several days or weeks. Among the places they shoulder record are any which they come into contact with, eg. visiting, letters from, support teams from, hear about on the radio, watch TV programmes about. At the end of the period they should map the places recorded, both individually and as a group/class. What do they find out from their evidence?

193 What to wear?

Divide the class into a number of groups. Each group is provided with the name of a holiday destination in another part of the world (ensure there is climatic variation). Each group has to 'pack a suitcase' with suitable clothing and must justify what is included. Each group should present the holiday wear in a display around a world map.

194 Sing a song of places

Collect a variety of songs with places in their titles or lyrics, eg. '24 hours from Tulsa', 'New York, New York', 'It's a long way to Tipperary'. Make a song map of the places mentioned.

195 Souvenir time

Children who have been finding out about a locality in another part of the world are asked to imagine that they are just about to return from visiting the area. They may pack up to five souvenirs. What would they bring back and why? Discuss what image of the place would be presented by the souvenirs.

196 From source to sale

Select a product. Find out where the raw materials needed come from, ie. where the product is made/grown and some of the places where it is sold in the UK and elsewhere in the world. Find out how the materials and product are transported. Map what is discovered on a national, continental or world map.

197 Where are they from?

In a local shopping area conduct a survey of pedestrians to find out what brings them to the area. Among the questions, ask where they come from and how they travelled to the area. Map the results of this study. What, if any, patterns emerge?

198 How would the children do it?

Individuals or groups develop ways to help other children learn about places around the world. The target age group can be specified (both older and younger children). The focus can be on being able to locate places and/or knowing something about specific places.

199 Place name origins

When was the name Great Britain first used? (In fact by James I in 1604 in a royal proclamation to show he was king of a united island, then adopted in the Act of Union in 1707.) Why is Holland also called The Netherlands? Why is Nigeria so named? Who gave a name to the Americas? What does Australia derive from? Select a variety of places (eg. country names and well–known cities) and set the task of finding out the origin and first use of the names.

200 Today's weather

Use weather reports from daily newspapers/TV sources about different parts of the world. Make daily weather maps using the data to show what it is like in particular locations.

201 Make a holiday brochure

Collect a variety of travel brochures about the same places from different travel companies. Select one of the locations and create your own travel brochure. Find additional sources to extend your knowledge of the area.

202 Regions

Find out which regions your locality is in: TV/radio regions, political regions, bus/rail regions, delivery region for a major store. How big an area comes into each of these regions? Identify criteria to define the home region for the locality. Map the region. How does it compare with the other regions that were identified?

203 Continental connections

What is the European/African/South American dimension in your school? Find out about what connections you have with another continent: What is in the school that comes from there? Does anyone speak any of its languages? Who has been on holiday there? Who has relatives who live there? Find out about the diversity of life and places in the continent. Mount a display to show what you have discovered.

204 Place debate

Divide children into groups. Each group has to make a case for their list of key places that everyone should know (which should be a list of no more than ten places). You could vary the arguments to specify people the list could be for: airline pilots, travel agents, politicians, and so on.

205 'Just a minute'

This is a variation on the popular radio panel game. Here are two versions. Give one child a feature or place to talk about for one minute, without mentioning the same points about it more than once. If there is hesitation or they repeat themselves the topic passes to the next child. Alternatively the child has to keep naming places in a continent, part of the world or country without repetition or hesitation. The area passes to a challenger when the child falters. Aids are not allowed. Depending on the experience and knowledge of the children, the time can be shortened, even to as little as ten seconds!

206 Pin the feature

This is similar to 'pin the tail on the donkey'. Provide a large outline wall map (eg. of a continent, country or the local area) and a variety of features and places on cards. The blindfolded child must attempt to pin the feature or place on the map with as much accuracy as possible! One variation, for children to whom the area is not familiar, is to play this without the blindfold. It can produce similar, hilarious, results!

207 Flat globe, flat map

Obtain an inflatable globe and a world map. Use them together to talk about what can be seen on the map and on the deflated 'flat' globe. Find features on both, eg. continents, oceans and seas. Discuss the differences and similarities between them. Inflate the globe and reconsider the differences and similarities.

208 Phone codes

Use the local telephone directory to find out the phone codes for a variety of cities in the UK, and countries and cities around the world. Map the phone codes and the places they are for (eg. a map which shows country boundaries but has phone code labels instead of country names).

209 Run, River, Run

Select a number of well–known rivers. Using an atlas, globe or wall map, find out their source and into which sea or ocean they flow and map them. Identify the countries the rivers flow through and towns or cities along their banks. Produce a strip map for the river. A similar activity can be undertaken using mountain ranges, deserts or major fault lines.

210 Designer place names

Make a wall map of Europe or another continent, on which you name all the countries. Find ways to make the names of the countries distinctive in their design. Link the name design to a characteristic associated with the country; use a variety of materials; use different type faces. (You cannot use the national flag.) Use this approach for naming features and places on a country map.

211 Parts of the world

You have heard of areas like 'The Near East', 'The Western World', 'The North', 'The Far East' and 'The Southern Hemisphere'. Make a list of these 'parts of the world' and attempt to map them. Find out which countries come into these areas. Do some countries come into several areas? Do areas overlap? Why are these 'parts of the world' so named? Develop a project to find out the origin and usefulness of these terms.

212 Spot check

Are you geographically literate? Are your friends? Is anyone else you meet? Ask what it means to be geographically literate. Generally it seems that people who are 'geographically literate' know the location of places. Do a spot check on your friends and other people. Ask them to locate a few places, just for fun. Later, try to patch up the relationship!

213 Postcodes

Find out the postcode for the school. What information does the postcode give? Discover postcodes for the local area of the school. Look out for postcodes on letters and in adverts. Map the location of these codes. Obtain a postcode atlas if possible and check the location of UK postcodes. Find out about postcodes in other countries (eg. zipcodes in the USA). Explain their purpose.

214 Flash countries

Put a map on the wall showing one continent. Make a set of flash cards each with the shape of one country from the continent. Children have to match the flash card to the country on the map by pointing it out or by naming it and stating its location (eg. by naming countries around it). Alternatively, write country names on the flash cards and the children point out the country shape on the map.

215 What makes a good locational question?

Encourage children to ask questions about the location of features and about the main features in particular parts or the whole world. They then use the questions on each other. Can they come up with suitable questions after prompting? (For example 'Where is Glasgow?', 'What are the largest countries in the European Union?', 'What are the main physical features of Asia?') They should provide a list of ten questions with answers. Having tried the questions out on other children, did they obtain the same answers? This may be either because some questions have only a single answer ('What is the capital of the UK?'), some can be answered correctly in various ways ('Where is Birmingham?'), or because it is a matter of opinion ('What are the three main physical features of the USA?'). Are these questions useful? Why?

216 All around the ocean

Select an ocean. Draw its shape (ie. the continental edges that mark it out). Around this shape write the names of the countries and other oceans which form its border (these could be written to form the shape that 'borders' the ocean).

217 'I left my heart in San Francisco'

To encourage children to name and locate places on maps, use an approach based on the song title, 'I left my heart in San Francisco'. Children should choose an item and say where in the world it was left. Link products to the country (eg. 'I left my nuts in Brazil'), use rhyming items (eg. 'I left my hoover in Vancouver') or refer to clothes (eg. 'I left my swimsuit in Monaco). There are plenty of alternatives. The places mentioned could be labelled with the item on a world, continent or national map.

218 Where next?

In a group of children, one child names a city, a second child then names a city which can be travelled to directly from the first by road, rail, sea or air (an atlas can be used). The third child finds another city in the same way. The round continues until someone makes an error by naming a city that cannot be reached directly, in which case the game begins again.

219 Place bingo

Make up a variety of 'place bingo cards' using the names of places and features instead of numbers. Write each feature on a separate card, put these into a container. Hand out the 'place bingo cards' to the class. Pick names of places and features from the container one by one and call them out. The first to call out 'bingo' (or 'mappo' or 'loco') correctly gets the prize of finding each of their places on an appropriate map! So does everyone else!

220 Building up a map

Provide the children with a blank map of a country, continent or the world. They should also have access to an atlas. Name features and places for them to mark on the map. Start with seas, then mountains ranges, rivers and plains/deserts, major towns and finally road/rail connections. As features are added discuss what is noticed about their relationship, eg where the mountains are, the relationship between the rivers and the mountains and into which seas the rivers flow, the links between towns and the road/rail system.

221 Collecting literary places

Use the books in the school or class library. Groups of children check through the books to find the names of real places. Lists are made and later transferred to maps to show the range of places 'in' the library. Consider the patterns that emerge. Does this raise questions about the purchase of books for the school or class?

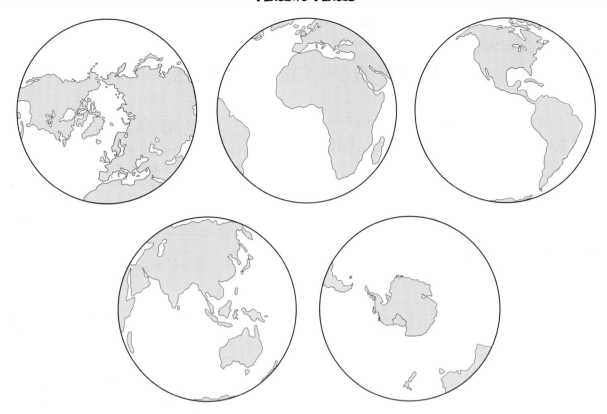

222 Hemispheres galore!

A photograph of the Earth from space shows one half of the globe – a hemisphere. Collect hemisphere views of the Earth centred on different continents and oceans. Atlases usually contain hemisphere views. Find out where they show. Can children name the key global features at a glance? Can they find the views on a globe? They can turn an inflatable globe to match the view shown in a photo or drawing.

223 The CD–ROM atlas

Purchase a CD–ROM atlas for the school. Encourage the children to use it to find out information about places in the news, or they have visited/heard of. Print out information to put into a scrap book or create a file, entitled 'Our World' using extracts from the atlas.

224 Shuttle–eye view

Give groups of children a globe, postcards showing views of the Earth from space and a toy space shuttle or rocket. Their task is to match the view on the card with the globe and to hold the shuttle to show where the 'photograph' was taken from. They should name the parts of the Earth that can be seen. (These could be marked on a map.) One variation is to place a floor or wall world map on a table and use a toy aeroplane to hold over features and places for the children to identify.

225 Where's ...?

Many globes, wall maps and atlas maps, as well as Ordnance Survey and street maps, are cluttered with the names of places. Give children a card bearing obscure name to find and provide them with no clues. In true *Where's Wally?* fashion they must find the name among the mass on the map or globe. Individual children or small groups could set this task for others, but they must able to find the name themselves!

226 Kept places, lost places

Give children a copy of the world map from the 1991 National Curriculum Geography Order and copy of the world map in the 1995 National Curriculum Geography Order. Ask them to make three world maps: one to show the places that are included on both maps, a second to show what has been introduced in the 1995 map and a third to show what has been dropped from the 1991 map. Set them the task of explaining the changes. Give them a time limit or they could be trying to work this one out forever!!

Appendix 1:
The locational framework for geography

The views of the Geography Working Group for England and Wales

The paragraphs below set out the argument put forward by the National Curriculum Geography Working Group in their final report, *Geography for Ages 5 to 16* (DES/WO, 1990), for the inclusion of locational knowledge in the requirements for geography in the National Curriculum.

6.11 Recent surveys have highlighted concern about the locational (place) knowledge of both school pupils and adults, and suggested that many people are worryingly ignorant of the most basic geographical facts. The Geographical Association in its discussion paper *Geography in the National Curriculum* asserted that: 'a National Curriculum for geography ... cannot and should not attempt to avoid the definition of reasonable expectations in this area of locational knowledge.'

6.12 We agree with this view and believe it to be unrealistic to suppose that much worthwhile understanding of geography can be attained without the acquisition of such basic knowledge. The names of places are embedded in everyday conversation and discourse, in newspaper, radio and TV items, and are part of the general culture which people need immediately to hand if they are to make any sense of the world around them.

6.13 We do not believe that the acquisition of basic knowledge is either a time–consuming or an irksome task. We expect this geographical base to be accumulated gradually through a variety of activities such as games, quizzes, computer work, the completion of jigsaws and the planning of journeys, as well as through the frequent incidental reference use of maps, atlases and globes. We see no reason for them to be given by list or learned by rote.

6.14 We considered carefully what places we should specify and reached our conclusions based on a number of criteria. These included: the need to provide elements of a basic spatial framework of the world, to which other pieces of information could be related; the size (both in area and population) of major countries; the size (in population) of major cities; the importance of certain places through their 'frequency of mention'; the importance of certain places for economic, political, historic, cultural or strategic reasons.

6.15 We think these place names – which we have specified on maps forming part of the programmes of study – are a realistic minimum to be acquired by most pupils by about the age of 14. On this foundation can be built the deeper knowledge acquired through case–studies and integrated area studies, and by information gained through studies of topical interest. In practice, we expect that pupils will also incidentally learn of other places which interest them, through the habits of regular use of map, atlas and globe which should be engendered.

(DES/WO (1990), *Geography for Ages 5 to 16*, DES/WO, pp. 47–8)

Criteria for selecting map content in England and Wales

In redrafting the content of the maps of the British Isles, Europe and the World, the School Curriculum and Assessment Authority used the following criteria:

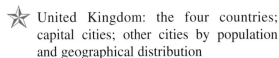 United Kingdom: the four countries; capital cities; other cities by population and geographical distribution

Europe: countries by area and population density but including all European Union countries; capital cities of countries named

World: countries by area, population and density, geographical distribution and gross national product; cities by population and geographical distribution

SCAA (1994), *National Curriculum 1995: Subject Seminars – Geography*, SCAA, Gg11 (Criteria for selecting map content)

Appendix 2:
Locational knowledge changes to the English and Welsh Geography Order maps from 1991 to 1995

Places and features introduced in the 1995 Order

i British Isles

- Cambrian Mountains
- Sheffield, Norwich, Nottingham
- compass rose

ii Europe

- Baltic Sea
- United Kingdom, Republic of Ireland, Sweden, Norway, Poland, Ukraine, Finland, Austria, Switzerland
- London, Dublin, Stockholm, Oslo, Warsaw, Kiev, Vienna, Bern, Luxembourg
- compass rose

iii The World

- Oceania, Atlantic Ocean
- Italy, France, Germany, Algeria, (Russian Federation)
- San Francisco, Paris, Seoul
- compass rose, scale bar (Equator)

Places and features removed from the 1991 Order

i British Isles

- Southampton

ii Europe

(nil)

iii The World

- Australasia, Southern Ocean, South Atlantic Ocean, North Atlantic Ocean, Caribbean Sea
- River Murray, River Darling, River Zaire (Congo), Zambezi River, River Ganges, River Volga, St Lawrence River, Colorado River
- Great Lakes
- Ghana, Kenya, Egypt, Algeria, Peru, Pakistan, Saudi Arabia, Israel, (USSR)
- St Petersburg, Singapore, Delhi, Accra, Lagos, Washington DC, Chicago, Toronto, Lima, Caracas, Jerusalem, Jakarta, Johannesburg

Appendix 3:
Map photocopy masters

The following seven maps are included for schools to reproduce. They can be used for some of the teaching ideas outlined in Chapter 3, or they can have places and features removed from or added to them before copying them to be used with your own teaching ideas.

Map 9 England and Wales

Map 10 Wales

Map 11 Scotland

Map 12 Northern Ireland

Map 13 The British Isles – United Kingdom

Map 14 Europe

Map 15 The World

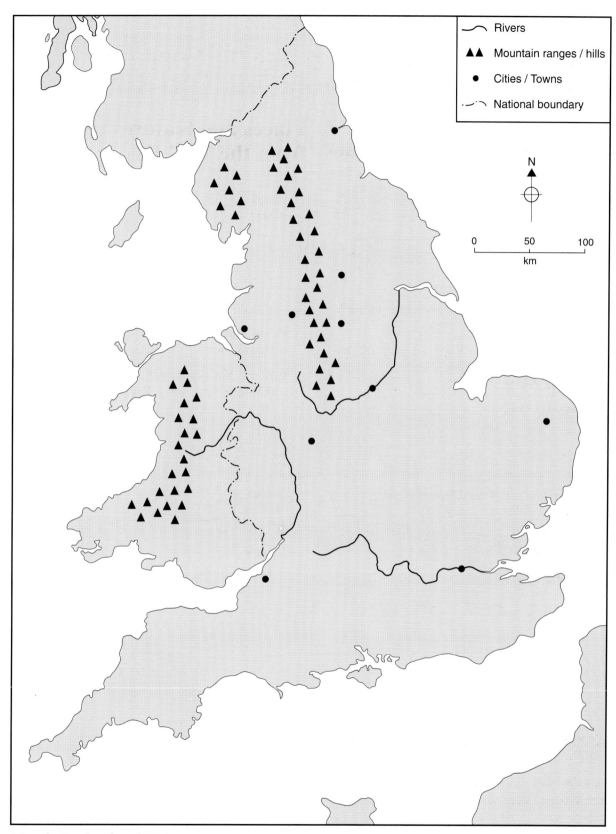

Map 9: England and Wales

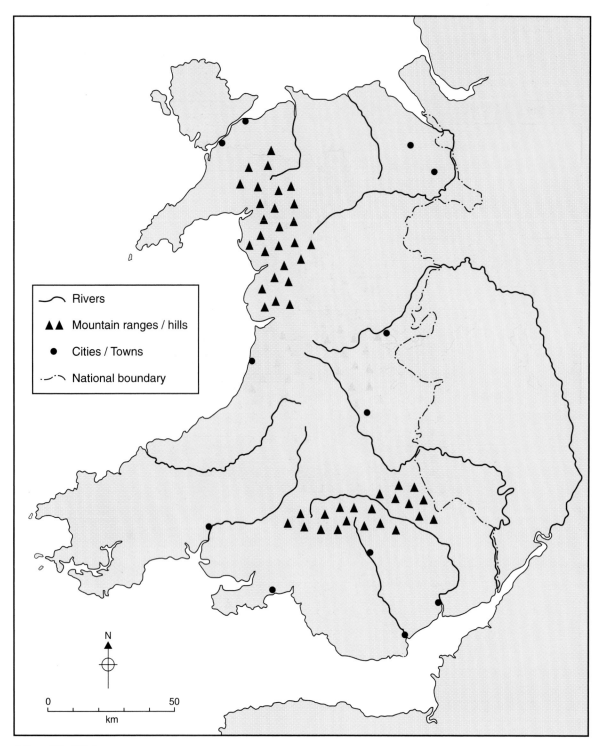

Map 10: Wales

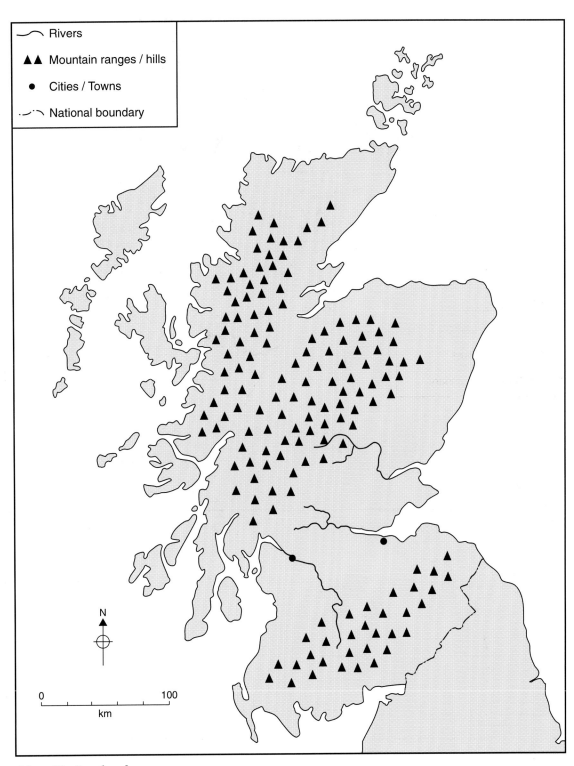

Legend:
- ⁀ Rivers
- ▲▲ Mountain ranges / hills
- ● Cities / Towns
- ⁀⁀ National boundary

N

0 ——————— 100
km

Map 11: Scotland

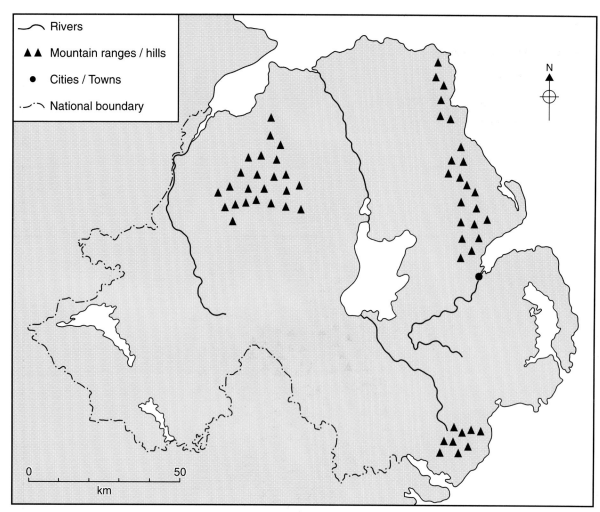

Map 12: Northern Ireland

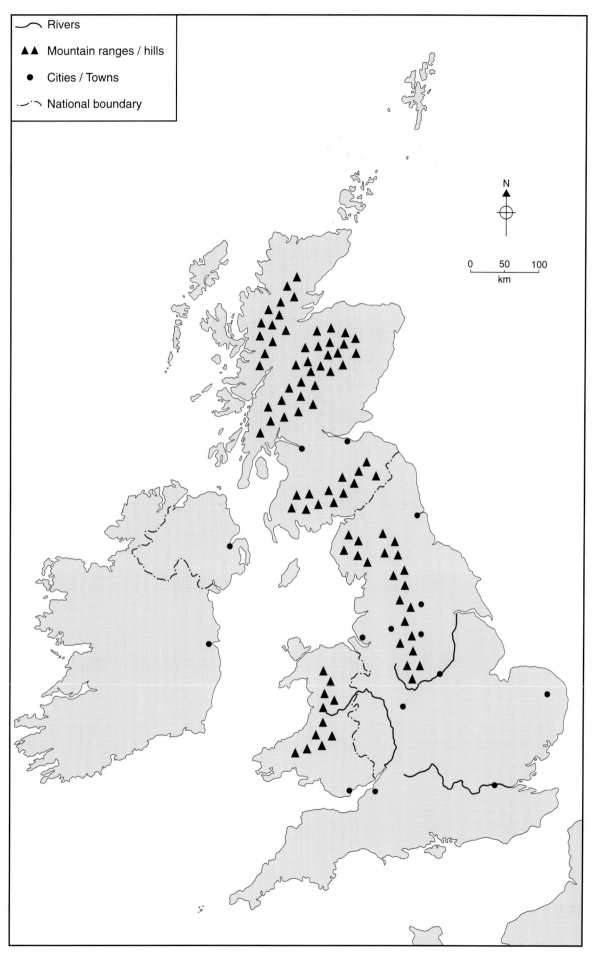

Map 13: British Isles – United Kingdom

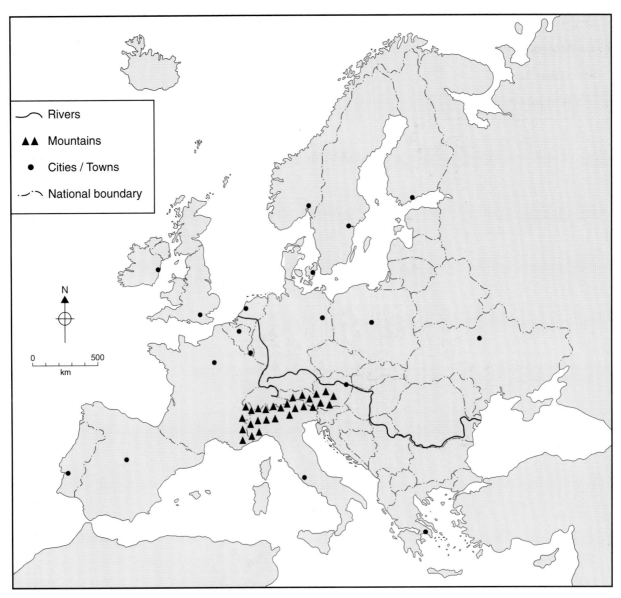

Map 14: Europe

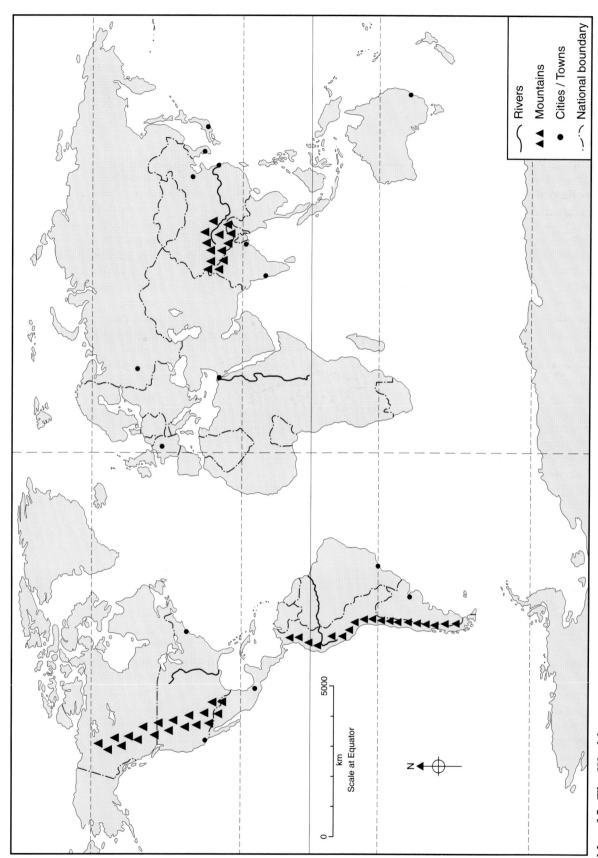

Rivers
Mountains
Cities / Towns
National boundary

5000

km

Scale at Equator

N

0

Map 15: The World

Index of ideas